BOLSHEVISM

AN INTRODUCTION TO SOVIET COMMUNISM

INTERNATIONAL STUDIES

of the

Committee on International Relations

University of Notre Dame

Bolshevism: An Introduction to Soviet Communism
by Waldemar Gurian

Christian Democracy in Italy and France
by Mario Einaudi and François Goguel

The Soviet Union: Background, Ideology, Reality
A Symposium Edited by Waldemar Gurian

Europe Between Democracy and Anarchy
by Ferdinand A. Hermens

IN PREPARATION

Panslavism
by Hans Kohn

The Foreign Policy of the British Labour Government, 1945-51
by M. A. Fitzsimons

Diplomacy in a Whirlpool: Hungary between Nazi Germany and
the Soviet Union
by Stephen Kertesz

The Social Ethic of German Protestantism: 1848-1933
by W. O. Shanahan

The Catholic Church in World Affairs
Edited by Waldemar Gurian and M. A. Fitzsimons

BOLSHEVISM

An Introduction to Soviet Communism

by

WALDEMAR GURIAN

University of Notre Dame Press
Notre Dame, Indiana

To the memory of Elizabeth Langgaesser
(d. 1950) who, knowing the Joy in despair, discovered the Light amidst the
darkness of our world.

PREFACE

This study does not pretend to give a detailed history and description of Bolshevism, its policies and institutions. It attempts only to reveal the basic features, the "essence" of that modern Communism which achieved power in Russia through the October revolution of 1917 and since has developed into a movement of world importance. This "essence" is not an abstract entity beyond time and space but is an historical-social force that influences, and is influenced by, historical-social developments. The political-secular religion of Bolshevism is not only a dogmatic doctrine but also the foundation of a very flexible practice. It combines utopian elements with cool consideration of power and its facts.

An introduction to Soviet Communism may help towards an understanding of the continuity as well as the changes in the Soviet regime and Soviet policies. Obviously, it cannot compete with special investigations and monographs, though it may occasionally contribute to a comprehension of the forest to which certain trees belong. The literature cited in the footnotes is kept to a minimum; the mention of books not published in English is generally avoided. A much shorter first draft of this study has appeared in German [pp. 8-36 of part IV of the *Wörterbuch der Politik*, Freiburg, Verlag Herder, 1951]. I am indebted to Verlag Herder for permission to use this version as a basis for the present study.

Of the many who aided me in the completion of my manuscript, I can mention only a few—Dr. F. T. Epstein (Library of Congress), Professors Barrington Moore (Russian Research Center of Harvard University), Hans Kohn (City College of New York), F. A. Hermens and M. A. Fitzsimons (University of Notre Dame) suggested changes and additions; all my colleagues on the Committee on International Relations of the University of Notre Dame showed a helpful interest in my work; the administration of the University of Notre Dame granted me time for research; Miss Ruth Almond made many very helpful suggestions and revisions; Mr.

Richard Kilmer read the first part of the manuscript; Professor Frank O'Malley of the Department of English of the University of Notre Dame made a final careful check; Doctor Michael Pap, research assistant for the Committee on International Relations, was of great help in translating the quotations from source-material; the manuscript would never have been completed without the competent typing of Miss Laura Beaulieu, secretary to *The Review of Politics*. For all shortcomings and errors the author alone is responsible.

WALDEMAR GURIAN

Notre Dame, Indiana
May 15, 1952

CONTENTS

INTRODUCTION

The name Bolshevism originated by chance. In London, 1903, at the second congress of the illegal Russian Social Democratic party, Lenin (born Vladimir Ilitch Ulianov) won a majority of votes on some issues, after several delegates, members of the Jewish Socialist Bund, withdrew, dissatisfied with the refusal to organize the party according to nationalities. Lenin's adherents were therefore called bolsheviki (*bolshinstvo* is the Russian word for majority) and his opponents mensheviki (*menshinstvo* is the Russian word for minority).[1] But Lenin's control of the leading committees was very precarious and shortlived. He did not succeed in dominating the party: many of his original followers left him. The father of Bolshevism was constantly obliged to reject attempts to restore party unity on conditions unacceptable to him. Finally, in 1912, a separate organization of the Bolsheviks was definitely established. Lenin created a separate central committee, of which Stalin (born Joseph Vissarionovitch Djugashvili), at this time a young professional revolutionary, became a member.

Only after the Bolsheviks had seized power in Russia through the October Revolution of 1917 (according to our calendar the Revolution took place in November) did they, in 1918, accept Lenin's proposal that they call themselves Communists so as to emphasize their difference from the moderate Social Democrats. They regarded themselves (and generally were regarded) as promoters of world revolutionary movements outside Russia. The creation of the Soviet regime in 1917, dominated by Lenin and his Party, was only a first step and a signal for the efforts to realize Socialism and Communism across the world. From the beginning the Bolshevik party was the leading group in the Third International (also called Communist International (Comintern)—founded in 1919 by Lenin). Its Moscow headquarters tried to control Communist movements everywhere; it regarded all Communist parties merely as its sections. The Comintern helped to bring about splits in Socialist parties outside Russia, as in 1922 its chairman Zinoviev

1

did at the congress of the German Independent Socialists of Halle. Its primary purpose was to create Communist groups under the permanent control and domination of Moscow.[2]

Upon the Bolshevik success in Russia the name Bolshevism, which previously had been known only to students of the Russian Socialist movement, was used universally. What appeared before 1917 to be a fanatic sect, ascribing to itself the mission of realizing socialism and of destroying existing society, had now become a real world danger. After the October Revolution the Bolsheviks seriously threatened to impose Communism on many countries, even on the whole world.

From the beginning of the Bolshevik movement in 1903, critics directed much the same kind of charges against Lenin and his policies[3] as were later advanced against the Soviet regime. Lenin was attacked for trying to establish "conditions of siege" in the party and an absolute personal dictatorship. Reading these accusations is like reading statements about Stalin and his almighty Politburo. Very early during the congress of 1903 the Bolsheviks made clear the anti-democratic basis of their policies. Plekhanov, later a bitter enemy of Lenin, but at that time cooperating with him, stated that the aim — the realization of socialism — would have to be attained by the use of any and all means; therefore it did not necessarily require democratic methods.[4]

A study of Bolshevism must consider both its Western and its Russian aspects. On the one hand, Bolshevism originated as a branch of a Socialist movement which had its roots in a western doctrine, Marxism; its development into Communism with all its worldwide appeal proves that it exercises a strong attraction for the world outside Russia. On the other hand, Bolshevism has been determined both in its peculiar features and also in its history by Russian environment and reality. Lenin was decisively influenced by the necessity of creating revolutionary organizations that could work under the restrictive conditions of the Tsarist regime.[5] Furthermore there is no doubt that the exigencies of keeping and expanding the power, that was seized in Russia, have shaped not only the policies but also the theories of Bolshevism.

INTRODUCTION

The first part of this book will attempt to disentangle these two aspects and at the same time to indicate how they influence each other, revealing how basic Bolshevik doctrine as developed by Lenin took over western Marxism with peculiar simplifications, accentuations and selections. These modifications empty Marxism of its sophisticated features and a refined awareness of problems; what remains is a political religion — a universal system formulated in slogans that seem to have a self-evident and logical character. This streamlined Marxism is widely accepted even outside Soviet Russia as a means of understanding complicated situations and of explaining the various intricate developments of our age (for example, world wars); it helps, too, in establishing a faith which substitutes for lost traditional beliefs, superseding — at least for a time — skepticism and nihilism.

The capacity of Bolshevik doctrine to seem both a key to the understanding of the present and a guide to action is of decisive importance. What matters less are its philosophical and economic contents — dialectical materialism, the labor theory of value that claims to prove scientifically the inevitable exploitation of labor under capitalism, and so on. Bolshevik doctrines are unoriginal simplifications and popularizations of Marx's thought. Therefore, Marxism as such,[6] though it is the historical background of Bolshevism, will not be analyzed in the present study, which is an attempt to explore the strange world created by Bolshevik theory and practice.

The second part of the book turns from the consideration of doctrine, to the Russian reality of Bolshevism, its origins and development, its rule and behavior; here typical policies and basic methods are emphasized in order to explain how the Soviet regime, despite all changes, maintained a fundamental continuity from Lenin to Stalin.

The third part will attempt to show why Soviet Communism has become a world power that owes its successes not only to such material factors as the strength of the empire under its control, but also to the exploitation of social and psychological crises in western society of the twentieth century. Here the analysis will show

3

how, despite its specific Russian features, Bolshevism continues to exercise a world influence; for it brings to full maturity seeds contained in the modern secularized world, which simultaneously it threatens to destroy. Bolshevism has not succeeded merely because of a conspiracy of ruthless men who employed systematically and dispassionately all methods useful for their aims. It has been successful because it brought to their logical conclusion tendencies and forces in our time accepted unconsciously even by many of those who sincerely believe that they are enemies of Soviet Communism. Bolshevism is a challenge to overcome the social and spiritual illness which made possible the successes of the Communist antireligious secular religion and its power machinery. Bolshevism can be defeated only when its true nature as a world menace is understood; this means that the shortcomings and errors of the society which it opposes are frankly recognized and remedied.

4

CHAPTER I

BOLSHEVISM AS SOCIAL AND POLITICAL RELIGION

The Basic Attitude

To comprehend the development, the successes and the dangers of the Bolshevist-Communist movement, it must be understood as a social and political secular religion, for it is not exclusively concerned with the conquest of power and the achievement of social and political changes. It demands absolute dominance over every realm of life — spiritual as well as secular. The Soviet regime does not regard itself simply as one among many possible regimes, but as a regime based upon a specific doctrine which corresponds to a necessary development in history and society. This doctrine allegedly is the only true guide to action, one destined to bring about justice for all men and to shape, besides, all human knowledge and behavior. What believers of traditional religions ascribe to God and what Christians ascribe to Jesus Christ and the Church, the Bolsheviks ascribe to the allegedly scientific laws of social, political, and historical development, which they alone know and have formulated in the doctrine established by Marx and Engels, Lenin and Stalin. Therefore, their acceptance of these doctrinal laws and of the policies called for by what they insist is the necessary development of society towards Socialism and Communism, can be characterized as a secular religion: earthly existence and the struggle to make it perfect are the sole aims of human life and of world history.

Bolshevism has always insisted that its basic doctrine, the so-called dialectical materialism, which has been presented in its official, definitive, obligatory form by Stalin himself,[7] alone provides the truth about the universe, men, history and society, and alone comprehends their development. The Bolsheviks regard all other doctrines and views as errors and heresies to be rejected and fought, as expressions of an outdated social order which defends the ego-

5

istic domination of a single class, as the sources of prejudices in opposition to objective scientific knowledge.

To deny God's existence is basic for Bolshevism. The aim of man and mankind is a self-sufficient, perfectly organized and effective "classless society" here on earth. Only in this society will man fully realize his nature and utilize all his potentialities. In this society all religion based upon belief in God will disappear as superfluous, for religion with its acceptance of God is, according to Bolshevism, only the expression of an imperfect social order and a denial of reason.[8] With Marx the Bolsheviks emphasize that the exploited, not yet aware of the real reasons for their exploitation, willingly escape to a dreamworld of religion and substitute for earthly justice (which is denied them and for which they are not yet willing to fight) a heavenly justice after death. The exploiters for their part use belief in God as a means to drug the masses, to keep them ignorant of the true condition of society, and so to prevent their fighting for justice here on earth. Religion is thus an opiate or, as Lenin put it, a "sivuschka" (a particularly low kind of alcohol).

The hatred which Bolshevism directs against religion — as expressed, for example, before the first World War, in the correspondence of Lenin with Gorki — shows that Bolshevism itself is a religion which deifies a purely immanentist secular development — a "religion" which replaces a transcendental God by a political and social order, the classless society. All history moves towards this society which gives meaning to all social and political development.

The Bolshevik rulers did not suppress all religious bodies at once because they believe that the fallacy and superstition of religion will disappear only with the rise of the perfect classless society. As long as society is imperfect and the aim of history is not achieved, traditional religions will necessarily exist, for they have their social roots in social and political backwardness. Bolshevik atheism is one of the various political and social religions of our time that deify various forces of history and social order.[9] An earthly force and an earthly order are at the center of all these secular religions, which deny either openly (as Bolshevism does) all acceptance of a transcendent order beyond *this* world, or which reinterpret traditional religions as a means of intensifying unlimited subservience to an immanent force, such as the Nordic race. Nazism deified domination by the superrace as the aim of society and history, as well as of all political activities. Here, racial character determines religion, and thus deprives it of all independent dignity.

The Belief in Development

The perfect, self-sufficient classless society cannot arise spontaneously, at just any moment, the Bolshevik doctrine emphasizes, but will emerge only after a long and inevitable development of society. The various stages of this development are determined by the prevailing means of economic production,[10] and the domination of the various classes corresponding to them. Capitalism, the system under which the bourgeois class controls society because it owns the means of production, will be overcome by the rise of the proletariat, the class which does not possess anything other than its own power to work and to produce.[11] Since class distinctions are based on the existence of private property, the proletariat is the class destined to abolish all classes, by taking exclusive control of society and by abolishing private ownership of the means of production. Under this "dictatorship of the proletariat," society will pass through two stages, the second of which will bring forth the Communist society.

The first stage, to be realized by the proletariat and the Communist party whose function is to formulate and carry out the real will of the proletariat, is called Socialism.[12] Here private control of the means of production has disappeared; the power of the bourgeois class is broken; but those who work are paid unequally according to their contribution to society. Socialism in the long run will result in such an abundance of production (because of the superiority of planning over capitalist anarchy and the disappearance of private profits resulting from exploitation) that the second stage, the purely Communist one, in which everyone can be rewarded according to his needs, will follow. At this Communist stage, the state or the political government (which Bolshevist doctrine defines as the instrument of systematic coercion in the interest of the domi-

7

nating class) will wither away. But the state must remain strong, it cannot wither away, according to Stalin, so long as the proletariat has not conquered the whole world, so long as the Soviet Union is surrounded by capitalist powers and capitalists who utilize for their purposes reactionary forces in the world and traitors inside the U.S.S.R.[13]

The Authoritative Ancestors: Marx and Engels

All basic Bolshevik doctrines are taken from the works of Karl Marx and Friedrich Engels. Bolshevism claims that it alone presents the correct interpretation and continuation of Marxism, the key to the right understanding of the universe and of history. To Bolshevism, dialectical and historical materialism are not subjective provisional formulations; instead they express the objective structure of all being and the eternal laws of all change.

Lenin always believed that he was a loyal orthodox revolutionary Marxist (though he claimed that he accepted Marxism not as a dogma but as a doctrine, a guide to action, which made it possible to learn from unexpected and unforeseen experiences and historical-social changes).[14] He regarded all his Socialist opponents as betrayers and falsifiers of the truth; the truth had been made accessible by the two great masters, Marx and Engels.

In his best known book, *State and Revolution* (1917), he tried to prove by quotations from Marx and, particularly, from Engels, the absolute necessity for a dictatorship of the proletariat. This dictatorship has as its aim to realize by any means, including mass terror and violence, the transformation of Capitalism into Socialism and Communism. In this book Lenin violently castigated Kautsky, the best known interpreter of Marxism before 1914, for having falsified the true revolutionary doctrines by sacrificing the dictatorship of the proletariat to his petty bourgeois belief in a peaceful democratic revolution.

True, Bolshevist propaganda today rarely mentions Marx and Engels, though they continue to be listed in bibliographies, together with Lenin and Stalin, as "classics" of Marxism. They are known to Soviet readers today almost exclusively because they are quoted

8

extensively by Lenin as his authorities. But this recession of Marx and Engels into the background does not change the fact that both the basic thought of Lenin and the fundamental manner of Stalin's approach are derived from them. In Bolshevism, as developed first by Lenin and further simplified by Stalin, there survives the basic views of Marx and Engels, which combine materialistic evolution with a belief in the necessary appearance of a perfect classless society through the victory of the proletariat and its party.

But the refined argumentation of Marx, the master of an extraordinary amount of knowledge in various fields, has disappeared. It has been replaced by easily memorized slogans and formulas which, although accompanied by verbal protestations against dogmatism, are used to build up a system and to explain everything. Despite the claims of Lenin and Stalin, under Bolshevism a Marxian scholasticism in the worst sense — one which replaces reasoning by quotations from authorities — has triumphed. Through Lenin, Bolshevism took over the basic elements of Marxism without any critical investigation, simply and utterly as an act of faith.

Marx claimed to have put the idealist Hegel back on his feet; different from the German philosopher, he regarded not ideas, but material economic forces as the basis of historical development. This development is accomplished not in a straight line, but in a dialectical process; each stage is the negation and at the same time the realization of the potentialities of the previous one (thesis, antithesis, synthesis). The whole is the explanation of its moments. There are other complications, for example, sudden accelerations and jumps which help to realize progress without going through all the preparatory stages. Marxian materialism is even more mysterious than Hegel's idealism, where determination by the absolute idea, the origin and aim of the development, explains the whole historical process. Marx, in a curious transformation, ascribes to matter the dialectical, progressive, meaningful forces of development. On the other hand, as Father Bochenski has correctly emphasized, materialism is used by Lenin and Stalin simply to signify a negation of idealism, that is, the acceptance of an objective reality.

The sociological and economical elements of Marx also have

9

been taken over and dogmatically simplified by Bolshevism. These include his belief in the role of the proletariat and socialization in history, in the dissolution of private ownership of the means of production as a consequence of industrialization, and in the necessary exploitation of labor under Capitalism. The materialism of Engels, often very crude, is influential, as is the Hegelian element of Marxism, the belief in a philosophy of history which explains the transitional, provisional character of all historical epochs and provides a definite end for all development. However, contemporary Bolshevism has not kept up Lenin's careful reading and interpretation of Hegel and has not followed his advice to study Hegel in order to understand Marx. Besides Hegel, whom he interpreted carefully, Lenin also thoroughly studied Clausewitz's famous treatise on war in order to adopt military methods for revolutionary activity. (That is why Bolshevism has been characterized — with some over-emphasis — as a combination of Marx and Clausewitz.)

The Authoritative Teacher: Lenin, the Anti-Imperialist

Stalin has often praised Lenin as the great teacher of the application of Marxian revolutionary tactics and methods to the age of monopoly-capitalism and imperialism. According to Lenin's book, *Imperialism, the Highest Stage of Capitalism,* written in 1916, imperialism (that is, a capitalism in decay, where monopolies have replaced competition) is characterized by the division of the world among a few rich and very powerful states, actually the agencies of capitalist and monopolistic trusts. Though they embrace "less than one-tenth" or "less than one-fifth of the inhabitants of the globe if the most generous and liberal calculations were made," they "plunder the whole world simply by clipping coupons." By exporting capital into their colonies and the territories controlled by them, the few capitalists who dominate these imperialist states make "enormous superprofits." [15] The struggle among the imperialists for new markets in order to increase their profits must result in constant crises in international relations and in wars. Lenin characterized World War I as "a war for the purpose of deciding whether the British or the German group of financial marauders is to receive the lion's share." [16]

This development of capitalism "into a world system of colonial oppression and of the financial strangulation of the overwhelming majority of the people of the world by a handful of advanced countries" is accompanied by a corruption of the labor movement. Some of the Socialist leaders and groups in the "advanced" countries are bought off by being permitted to acquire a share of the "superprofits." On the other hand, the international tensions and crises produced by imperialism accelerate, in turn, the rise of revolutionary movements which aim at replacing imperialist anarchy and exploitation by Socialism and Communism.

Though Lenin, as he admitted, was greatly influenced in his description of imperialism by the liberal, Hobson, and the moderate Socialist, Hilferding — he claimed to formulate the revolutionary tactics for our time, the "higest stage of capitalism." These tactics assume that the development of the various peoples and regions are unequal, but this very inequality can be exploited for revolutionary purposes. Therefore, it would be a mistake to rely on simple evolution without aggression and attack and to wait until a stage of capitalism, with elaborate industrialization and with proletarian masses, is achieved. The opposition of the bourgeois class to the outmoded privileges of the feudal nobility or of colonial masters no less than the movements of the masses against the nobility and the bourgeoisie must be utilized: bourgeois and Socialist revolutions can coincide and can be pushed forward at the same time. It is especially necessary to revolutionize colonial regions even though they are politically, socially, and economically backward — for their aspirations to political independence and national self-determination can be used by the Communists to arrive at power and to destroy world capitalism.

These theories of imperialism, and the accompanying claim of Bolshevism-Communism to end international exploitation and war have exercised a tremendous influence. Even many who rejected Communist objectives, took over the thesis that all colonial rule, all the privileges of Europe and the United States must be terminated as unjust and oppressive. Lenin's anti-imperialism helped to stimulate Asiatic nationalisms, though later many Asiatic leaders turned against the Soviet Union. Lenin's theory of the unequal degree of the development of countries made it possible to use backward countries, as the weakest links in the imperialist chain, for revolutionary purposes. This theory also served to justify the Bolshevik conquest of power and the Bolshevik policy in a Russia which had not yet become a fully industrialized capitalist realm with a proletariat as the most numerous class. Lenin's anti-imperialism not only helped to portray the Bolsheviks as opponents of war — were not all wars products of imperialism? — but to defend the aggressive tactics of the Marxists in their struggle for power. It was not necessary to wait until the development Marx prescribed had reached a mature stage; by exploiting every crisis and revolutionary situation, power could be seized and even the development of backward agrarian countries could be forced in the right direction — toward the Socialist-Communist world revolution.

The Emphasis Upon Terror

In contrast to the moderate Socialists, whom they attack as opportunists and traitors because they accept a peaceful gradual development of society, the Bolsheviks emphasize the necessity of violence. Force and violence, they maintain, have been used in all periods of history to establish new social orders and are therefore needed to accelerate the emergence of Socialist and Communist societies. In the dictatorship of the proletariat force and violence are utilized, not for personal subjective reasons, but to facilitate objective social processes. The Soviet rulers are not concerned with punishing guilty people or satisfying feelings of hate and revenge; they apply force and violence to push forward an allegedly necessary and meaningful development which reached a decisive stage when the Bolshevik party seized power in Russia.

When written law was introduced in the Soviet regime, Lenin emphasized the need to remember that terror, merciless terror, against all enemies of the Soviet regime must remain the basis of procedure, and that the crucial importance of terror must not be obliterated by legalistic formulations.[17] This explains why it would be useless to judge the Soviet regime on the basis of legal or constitutional texts. Judgment on such a basis would mean falling into the trap of constitutional illusions against which Lenin himself protested in his articles of 1917.[18]

Acceptance of mass terrorism as an unavoidable weapon explains why the Stalin constitution of 1936, with its system of guarantees for individual rights, did not prevent the seemingly cynical disregard of those rights whenever the party leadership decided it had to supersede them. Despite all legal and constitutional limitations, terrorism remains justified if the situation and the stage of development of society require it. And terrorism means the unrestrained use of force, force determined exclusively by considerations of power and justified by the objectives towards which it is applied.

The Party

The views of the nature and the role of the Party are especially characteristic of Bolshevism. They can be regarded correctly as elaborations of some passages in the *Communist Manifesto,* written by Marx and Engels in 1848.[19] There the Communists are described as the central movers, the vanguard of the proletarian movement. They know the direction this movement must take if it is to fulfill its historical mission in accordance with the laws of the development of society. The Communists are the great men of Hegel, possessed of the right historical awareness, whose actions are right because they correspond to the stage of historical and social development just reached.

It was because they differed basically about the character and the role of the party, that the Bolsheviks and Mensheviks split.[20] For the Mensheviks the Party was a loose community of persons sharing the same political views. Their concept of the Party was not different from that usually held in the Western liberal and democratic world, where a party does not claim total domination of the life of its members; rather it enlists them solely for limited political purposes.

For Lenin, on the contrary, the Party was a strictly disciplined and organized group led by professional revolutionaries ready to fight for accession to power by every means, and deeming their party membership as the determining force of their whole existence. For Lenin the Party was a group of believers in a specific world outlook and doctrine which they accepted as *the* unquestionable truth, a guide to all theory as well as all practice. Of course, Lenin believed it self-evident that his interpretation of Marxism alone was exclusively true, that it corresponded to the real will of the masses. Even before the London Congress of 1903, when Bolshevism came into being, he denounced bitterly the opportunist "trade unionist mentality," as concerned only with the immediate issues of daily life. Instead he propounded a true revolutionary consciousness that preserved the orthodox Marxian doctrine of political-social revolution and was not satisfied with social reforms, improvement of living conditions, and so on. In Lenin's eyes, all Socialist politicians, labor and union leaders hostile to his views were traitors seduced by the capitalists and imperialists with the aid of their superprofits. He polemicized mercilessly against those Socialists who disagreed with him and therefore with his Party — that is, *the* Party. The tone of his language shows that he had not the slightest doubt that he and his organization were always right.

This dogmatic attitude derives from Marx and Engels. Engels compared Marx with Darwin.[21] What Darwin did for nature, Marx did for society: he discovered the laws of its development. Marx and Engels regarded themselves, their correspondence reveals, as infallible judges of men and unerring interpreters of historical events. Accordingly, Bolshevism claims to possess in the Party the authoritative organ for the interpretation of the true doctrine, for its application to changing circumstances, as well as for its correct evolution under conditions not yet known to its originators; the Party determines, too, the orthodoxy and therefore the value of its members. As the most authoritative obligatory textbook, *History of the Communist Party of the Soviet Union,* puts it: "The power

14

of the Marxist-Leninist theory lies in the fact that it enables the Party to find the right orientation in any situation, to understand the inner connection of current events, to foresee their course and to perceive not only how and in what direction they are developing in the present, but how and in what direction they are bound to develop in the future." [22]

Occasionally the Communist Party has been compared to a religious order. This comparison overlooks two facts: religious orders do not claim domination over all mankind, nor do they aim at the realization of a specific social and economic order here on earth. However, if the differences in the basic world outlook and aims are disregarded, and the comparison is strictly limited to the relations of members to superiors, the party and the religious order do appear to have this much in common: the members of each are obliged to obey their superiors, and this obedience is based on the idea of serving exclusively a true world outlook. But in the religious order obedience is limited by moral considerations, whereas for the Bolshevik Party such considerations do not exist — any means is proper for its aims. The goodness of the aim, and the need to fight for it in conformity with the orders of those who know everything about the correct theory and practice, warrants every means. The question of a conflict between ends and means cannot be raised in a Party whose leadership claims that it can foresee an inevitable future.

For its believers the Communist Party appears to be the instrument of an unavoidable social development, whereas critical outsiders look upon it as a group of ruthless activists cynically justifying their deeds by an "infallible" social doctrine. In all its actions the Party sees itself as executing only the laws of an objective and necessary development. The Communist Party, at least in its official views, does not accept a policy of making adventurous experiments, like the so-called "left" Communists who, as Lenin put it, intoxicate themselves with pseudo-revolutionary oratory.[23] Nor is the Party willing to become the victim of a mechanical adaptation to existing, that is unchangeable and definite, conditions. This attitude is characterized as opportunism or as a betrayal of belief in the ultimate aims — genuine Socialism and Communism. Such a betrayal is attributed by Communists to the moderate Socialists, who reject the dictatorship of the proletariat under the leadership of the Communist Party and therefore end up as helpers of Capitalism and Imperialism.

Utopianism and Power Politics

At first glance Bolshevism seems to be a system of rigid concepts, a doctrine which puts reality into a terminological straightjacket. Over-all developments of society, Bolshevism believes, are accomplished by iron necessity — though their details are not known in advance. They must end in the full realization of human nature and, therefore, of the freedom of the classless society; it is assumed that a change in property relations will achieve the perfection of society and of the behavior of men. Lenin and Stalin, Bolshevik doctrine insists, have brought the application of the Marxian doctrine up to date by learning from the experiences of the twentieth century and from the exercise of a power obviously lacking to Marx and Engels.[24]

Despite its apparent rigidity, Bolshevik doctrine is very flexible, because of its use of dialectics. The truth, in dialectical processes, is realized by its passing through various periods, uncovering its various aspects; the synthesis is reached only by the accumulation of all partial experiences and achievements corresponding to a particular historical moment. The proletariat, for example, takes over all bourgeois progress and utilizes it for the development of Socialism. The bourgeois thus is a class wholly determined by the past, not able to understand the present; therefore, it is necessarily reactionary and an evil hindrance to progress. It is assumed that the Party is always able to find the correct way to progress and advancement. But this correct way can be realized only through complicated and violent struggles with the most dangerous external enemies and internal foes. Those who betray the true way either are influenced or bought by representatives of the capitalist-bourgeois world and include undisciplined and cowardly persons within

16

the Party itself. The correct way — to make matters more complicated — is rarely a direct one: many detours are invariably necessary; and the Party must retrace its steps in order to be able to advance later, as Lenin emphasized.[25]

This doctrine, the omniscient Party insists, is not merely a collection of abstract statements without reference to specific historical circumstance, but is definitely related to concrete situations. The Bolsheviks insist that practice and theory form an indissoluble unity; and this unity is constantly realized and renewed by the authority of the Party leadership and the obedience required from followers.

The combination of a dialectically justified, flexible power politics on the one hand, and a doctrinaire utopianism on the other, explains both the ambiguity and the cynical practice of Bolshevism in action. Old Party members suddenly are cast in the role of traitors if they do not submit to the victorious Party leadership or if their condemnation seems useful for the Party's maintenance and expansion of power. If the obligations of power demand it, retreats are permitted. At such times it is said that historical development was not yet advanced enough, that possibilities and chances were overestimated.

The laws of dialectics — for example, the development by sudden jumps after a long slow process and the unique character of such jumps — are utilized to justify pauses, retreats, cooperation with enemies of yesterday in order to fight the more dangerous adversaries of today, the abandonment and destruction of allies who under new situations become enemies and parasites and must be immediately liquidated. All these maneuvers and changes are not casual products of the Machiavellian mentality of Stalin or of other Bolshevik leaders. They derive necessarily from the basic principles of Marxism-Leninism. On the one hand, there is the belief in the Party's knowledge of the ends towards which the development of society moves necessarily. On the other hand, there is the assumption that all epochs before the rise of the classless society have a transitory-provisional character: what is progressive today becomes reactionary tomorrow. Only the Party knows the right way to the

17

final aim. Only the Party always makes the right distinction between reactionary and progressive forces. And only the Party knows the tactics which correspond to the conditions of the moment and must therefore be applied. The Party, unlike sufferers from the disease of radical utopianism, does not underestimate difficulties. But the Party does not overestimate them as do the opportunists who lack belief in the necessity of a constant fight for progress and confuse temporary provisional gains with definite and lasting results.

The Bolshevik Faith

The Party's claim that its decisions are always both useful and absolutely true gives the impression that the Party is simply a group of cynics anxious to maintain and increase their power at any price. But such a view underestimates important sources of Bolshevism's strength; the deterministic but at the same time ethical belief in the necessary evolution of society toward the final realization of freedom, justice and humanity justifies and requires the unlimited power of the Party. The definition of freedom, justice and humanity is based on fundamental views about the nature of man and society. Lenin in his *State and Revolution* announces that the dictatorship of the proletariat will make all work a pleasure, and thus make coercion, and therefore the state, superfluous.[26] Following Marx he believes that the perfection of human nature and the realization of freedom depend upon the socialization of the means of production, which is of course a purely external-organizational change. These basic errors still make a great impression on many people who are looking for clear decisions and a new "faith" to give them clear "standards" for action as well as "guaranteed" promises for the future. What is decisive for these people is the pretense of the Bolshevist-Communists to know not only the over-all development of society but also the meaning of any given present situation. The loss of certain transcendent religious beliefs results in the acceptance of pseudo-certainties in *this* world, in its history and social development.

The Bolsheviks assert that they alone really stand for true justice and freedom and that they also know how to realize them. This

18

claim gives new strength again and again to the demands of the Party for power and domination. For example, a favorite point in the current Bolshevik propaganda program ascribes exclusively to the Communist Soviet regime and its friends the only true opposition to aggressive war and the only sincere will to maintain peace, for they alone know not only what imperialism is but also how to liberate mankind from it.

Such propaganda is useful to confuse opponents and to strengthen fanatical obedience in the ranks of the believers in Communism. The non-Communist world is always allegedly preparing aggression, whereas the Soviet Union — in all its policies, armament development, and attempts at expansion — is always interested in its own defense, eager only to preserve and maintain peace. On the one hand, Communists declare that it is possible to maintain the peaceful co-existence of the Communist and Capitalist worlds, and that this possibility determines the actions of the Soviet Union. They claim, on the other hand, that there are constant threats of war, from Capitalist powers. These powers are necessarily opposed to a genuine peaceful development which must end with their defeat, for the Capitalist world will disintegrate. The Capitalists are necessarily obliged to talk of "crises" and "attacks" to divert attention because they are unable — according to Bolshevism — to find satisfactory solutions for the contradictions of their system. It does not matter that many facts obviously do not fit into the Communist scheme. For the scheme itself, as we have seen, determines what the facts are and how they are to be interpreted.

The basis and significance of Bolshevism can be fully understood only when we realize that it is more than a political, economic or sociological doctrine. It is also a political religion maintaining that it knows the nature of the universe and of society, both in structure and in development.

The political religions which have played such a great role in the nineteenth and twentieth centuries replace transcendent beliefs by immanent ones.[27] There is for them only one world, the world of political and social action: they explain away traditional religion as the expression of social imperfection and human ignorance which forces men to escape into a heavenly world of their own fantasies, for Marx took over from Feuerbach the thesis that God has not created man but that man has created God. Sometimes these political religions utilize religious beliefs and concepts — this is true of Nazism and Fascism — to strengthen and glorify such this-worldly realities as *the* party, the elite of the nation, or a race. The political religions of the nineteenth and twentieth centuries replace the Kingdom of Heaven, the City of God, based upon union with God and the realization of an order established by God, by a purely immanentist this-worldly aim, the result of a naturalist development or the expression of a purely human-natural energy and group.[28] The struggle towards this aim — the Marxian classless society — or the elite or master race of Fascism and Nazism, determines the meaning and direction of the whole of human existence. Therefore, all such political-social activity has a pseudo-religious character, has its end in itself, is no longer in the service of a higher order determining and directing all human life and activity. Political-social programs assume the significance of religious creeds; membership in *the* party becomes as important as membership in the Church (or any group established by the Will of God) is for religious people.

All political and social tensions are thereby tremendously exacerbated. This explains the inclination to regard contrary political views as heretical doctrines based upon antisocial attitudes and to deal with "heretical" opponents as vicious enemies who must be annihilated and liquidated. The Church is not only replaced by the Party; the Party has become something more than the Church. For the Party not only determines the right beliefs — it also guides the attainment of the true aim of life here on earth (and there is no other aim); it dominates the creed as well as the conduct of life. The proletariat, in the eyes of Marx and Engels, is the "redeemer," the class with a unique liberating role, fulfilling every end of mankind.[29]

But it must be noted that in practice the Soviet Union, the Bolshevik state which is the instrument of the party, has been substituted for the proletariat. This state is the necessary means for the realization of the role ascribed to the proletariat and its dictatorship. All decisions for or against the political religion are regarded and evaluated as decisions for or against the Soviet Union. Only with the Soviet Union can the earthly paradise be reached. Without it or against it there is only the abyss of a meaningless existence opposed to the right historical trends. Hostile to the Soviet Union are only those helpless and vicious elements which will inevitably be overrun by the development of society and are, consequently, destined to disappear.

The Foundations of the Cynical-Amoral Practice

Bolshevism can be characterized as a politico-social religion based upon belief in a necessary economic-materialistic development and in a naturalistic-immanentist atheism; this belief assumes the self-sufficiency and infinite perfectibility of human nature. It is precisely this belief which makes Bolshevik practice cynical and amoral. In dealing with the enemy anything that may defeat him, is allowed. The enemy — or whoever Bolshevism says its enemy is — cannot assert any rights; as soon as he is weak enough he can and must be destroyed. Whoever opposes the Soviet Union and its leadership must be fought and liquidated. If the masses anywhere oppose the Communist Party and the Soviet Union, they prove only that they do not know their own will and their real interest. All kinds of violence and propaganda are justified if they are in the service of the aim, which is the classless society, whose coming depends upon the existence and power of the Soviet Union.[30] Lenin justifies explicitly the direction of mass terror against hostile classes, but he rejects terror against outstanding individuals, that is assassination of the Tsar, his ministers, generals, and so on. For such actions, he maintains, are politically inefficient and express a romantic belief that the power of a person can direct and determine objective trends.

Marx and Engels developed systematically a political-social religion by combining belief in a social perfectibility (taken over from utopian socialists), an historical-dialectical determinism learned from Hegel, a naturalistic-atheistic view of men, and scientific economic analysis. This political-social secular religion became a

21

force which determined and shaped world politics through the Bolshevik seizure of power in Russia. Characteristic of Bolshevism is its strong emphasis upon the utopian pseudo-religious elements of Marxism, particularly its belief in the eventual appearance of the classless society, which will result from a dictatorship of the proletariat and its "avant-garde," the Party.

In this utopian pseudo-religion, the scientific-critical elements, which would militate against revolutionary action and the merciless exploitation of power, recede, though they are employed as proofs of the infallible character of the basic method. It is not by chance that Bolshevik theorists have not presented any new economic analyses, that they have only offered interpretations of Marx-Engels (for example, Lenin in his *State and Revolution*) or have applied Marxian concepts to new historical developments (for example, Lenin in his studies on imperialism, or in a more primitive way, Stalin in his emphasis upon a strong state during the period of the dictatorship of the proletariat). They always try to show that the Marxian method can be applied to reach an understanding of new experiences and situations and that Marxian basic concepts must always serve as the leading ones. If Stalin repeats Lenin's protestations (of 1917) against the dogmatism of the pseudo-Marxist, he still does not surrender the fundamental principles; he applies them only to the needs of the moment and the new situation. In extreme cases the Bolsheviks admit that practical reinterpretations are necessary in the face of unexpected developments, for example, the rise of imperialism without free competition, or the Bolshevik seizure of power with accompanying demands in practical politics. Lenin knew that the Soviet regime could not last without neutralizing the peasants by giving them land belonging to estate owners, and thus he was willing to take over a non-Marxian program.

This fundamental attitude explains the striking combination of a rigid dogmatic terminology with a flexible cynical practice which is characteristic of Bolshevik behavior and propaganda. All political detours and deviations can be justified by an appeal to the need for a realistic appraisal of existing conditions and of the prevailing relations of forces. The "heaven," the end of history, the classless society of Communism will arrive anyhow, necessarily. Therefore, patience is required; one must wait a little longer. In the transitory period any action may be taken by those who know the truth and the end — and work for them. For it is they alone (according to the official doctrine) who bring about the realization of the end: because they are fighting for the true end, nothing that they do can be wrong. In the future the state will wither away, but to make possible this withering away, the power of the state must be increased while preparing for this eventuality. The classless society without coercion promised for the far away future, justifies the present rise of the totalitarian Soviet state as the proper instrument for the millenium.

CHAPTER II

THE SOVIET REALITY OF BOLSHEVISM

The expansion of Bolshevism into a world power cannot be explained exclusively by its character as a secular political religion. In order to understand its historical role, many questions about its Russian background must be raised. Why did Bolshevism originate as a political movement in Russia alone? [31] How far has Bolshevism been influenced by the fact that in Russia it became first a political power, the master of a state and its apparatus? Has Bolshevism changed completely, having obtained control of Russia? How is it to be explained that Marxism, originating in the West, became, in its revolutionary interpretation, the doctrine in whose name domination over Russia was achieved? Through what forces and circumstances has the Soviet regime survived, whereas outside Russia, in the Soviet satellites — with the exception of Red China — the Communists have been unable to conquer and to maintain power without help from occupying Soviet armies? [32]

The analysis of the relationship of Bolshevism to Russian history and environment illuminates the lasting features as well as the changes in the Soviet regime. What are the permanent elements and forces of the Bolshevik system which persist beneath all changes and adaptations to new political and social conditions? [33] Why does Bolshevism, despite its connection with Russia, retain a universal appeal to groups and movements outside the Soviet Union?

The Role of the Radical Intelligentsia

Bolshevism came into the world as a child of the Russian radical intelligentsia.[34] This group developed during the nineteenth century. It was the product of the contradiction between the Tsarist absolutist-bureaucratic regime on the one side, and the acceptance of the West, since the reign of Peter the Great (ruled from 1689-1725), as a standard and example for the leading and educated strata of Russian society. During the eighteenth century the rise of

25

a society in Russia influenced by the West did not create active opposition against Tsarist absolutism: for at this time enlightened absolutism also prevailed in Western Europe. But after the French Revolution absolutistic regimes began to be outmoded in the West, while liberal and democratic political ideas and institutions came to be regarded as modern and to exercise a practical influence. The educated classes of Russia, first predominantly officers and aristocrats, and later, after the 30's persons of various social origins, the so-called *raznotchintsy* (physicians, students, writers, members of the civil service, etc.), tried in many cases to apply these ideas to Russian society. Therefore, just because they accepted the Westernization definitely imposed under Peter the Great, they regarded the existing Tsarist regime as a contradiction of modern trends, and as unjust because it did not adopt western democratic, liberal and socialist thought and policies. Some members of the educated classes like the Slavophiles, Kireyevsky and Chomiakov, opposing the turn to the West and away from Old Russia, rejected the bureaucratic regime which predominated after the foundation of St. Petersburg. They regarded it as too much determined by non-Russian elements and they wanted a return to an old-Russian tradition. Therefore, even the conservative intellectuals were opposed to the existing regime. True, they did not reject it in the name of liberalism, democracy and revolution, but in the name of an idealized past.

The Westerners (Belinsky, Herzen, Bakunin) — who can be regarded as ancestors of Bolshevism, though they are, of course, not responsible for it — were inclined to accept the most radical of Western ideas, from anarchism to socialism, despite their dislike for the egoistic Germans (expressed by Bakunin) and the decadent, philistine, self-contented European bourgeois (expressed by Herzen). These ideas were taken over by their Russian believers in the purest form, with all implications and consequences. They appeared in Russia not as theories and philosophical speculations, but as living forces destined to determine life and action. Even if Russian intellectuals like Tchernyshevsky, Pisarev,[35] and Dobrolyubov, men of the sixties — in accordance with the Western example — became utilitarians, materialists, and believers in a positivistic scientism, denying metaphysics and religion, they did it with a most intense faith and enthusiasm, giving a religious character to their anti-religious, crass naturalistic and anti-idealistic attitudes.

This attitude, well-characterized as an anti-religious religion, was fostered by the impossibility of checking the accepted ideas and ideals in the reality of political and social experience; the existing Tsarist absolutist regime did not permit that. Despite all measures against radicals and radical writings, literary discussions could and did take place. Political and social ideas and utopias were uncritically accepted, because those accepting them were not restrained by any traditions, or impeded by any practical considerations. Intellectuals and publicists took all radical denunciations of existing conditions and utopias much more seriously than their Western teachers and masters. The dominant Tsarist regime was despised as unjust, inhuman and reactionary, as opposed to all progress. So the inclination to believe in the political and ethical necessity of accomplishing a change by revolution developed among the intelligentsia with the exception of those who, like Dostoyevsky after his sojourn in Siberia, became orthodox Christians and nationalist conservatives and developed feelings of superiority towards the West.[36]

This belief in revolution to be followed by a utopia was held without any recognition of possible impeding historical forces and shaped the basic attitudes of the Russian intelligentsia until the rise of Bolshevism to power. This is shown by the famous criticism of the mentality of the Russian intelligentsia in the symposium *Signposts* (Vechy),[37] published before World War I. The critical-enlightened mentality rejecting religious traditions and spiritual ideas remained influential among the intelligentsia until the revolution of 1917, in spite of all attacks by those who, like Berdyaev and Bulgakov, tried to overcome this narrowminded humanitarian and utilitarian progressivism. The conservative writers, though often represented by much more gifted and profound thinkers, V. V. Rozanov, for example, were clearly on the defensive in the eyes of many educated Russians. They were hampered by accusations that they defended the brutal, reactionary Tsarist regime with its bureaucracy, its clumsy and inhuman nationalism; that they disregarded the ethical and modern concepts of democratic radicalism and socialism which ought to be transplanted to Russia. If intellectuals such as Berdyaev tried to unite religious thought with the rejection of reactionary policies they were regarded as more or less gifted exponents of a paradoxical attitude. Belinsky had expressed, though in somewhat exaggerated formulas, the rejection of the Church by the average member of the intelligentsia when he opposed, in 1847, to Gogol's pleas for Christian humility his famous statement: "Russia sees her salvation not in mysticism nor in asceticism or pietism, but in successes of civilization." The radical intellectuals regarded the Orthodox Church as the tool and justifier of the dominant reactionary Tsarist regime incompatible with science and preventing true education.

Only after the middle of the nineteenth century did the radical intelligentsia attempt to win the masses over to a movement directed against the Tsarist regime. The first revolutionary effort made by the Decembrists, in 1825, was fomented by circles of officers and aristocrats without popular support. In the second half of the reign of Alexander II (1855-1881) the radicals realized that a literary movement addressed to intellectuals, particularly students, could not obtain practical results. Instead, they pinned their hopes on terror and on the peasants. Some expected that attempts against the lives of high officials and the Tsar himself would be a signal for a revolution of the masses. Others held the romantic belief that the Russian peasant for whom village communities without individual land property were characteristic, had a particular affinity for socialism. An old opponent of Tsarism like Herzen, a Westerner, became, through this belief, almost a Slavophile, though he rejected all religious foundations for his claim that the Russian people had a particular mission to realize a non-bourgeois society.[38]

Narodniki and Marxists

This sentimental-utopian attitude was opposed from the 1880's on, especially by Russian Marxism (spread first among emigres) of which Plehkanov was the most outstanding representative. Lenin's older brother held on to the belief that terroristic actions would be successful and paid for this opinion with his life; he was executed after his capture in the act of preparing an attempt on the life of Alexander III.[39] But Lenin himself, as a high school student, joined a Marxist study circle and became convinced that the revolutionary results of social and economic developments could not be replaced by individual heroic acts. Marxian doctrine was for Lenin, a typical Russian Marxist, a certain unshakable faith, corresponding to the results of truly scientific inquiry. The Marxian thesis about the necessary revolutionary mission of the industrial proletariat was defended by Lenin against those who ascribed a revolutionary role to the peasants or who emphasized the role "of critically thinking intellectuals" (Lavrov, Mikhailovsky) rejecting the attitude of scientific determinism (Narodniki). It was the Marxian belief that in Russia, too, capitalism was developing. Young Lenin's polemical writings against the Narodniki were crowned by his study of the *Rise of Capitalism in Russia* (1897), written in his easy Siberian exile; the Tsarist police finally had stopped his revolutionary propagandistic and organizing activities among the workers of St. Petersburg. (Young Lenin had, almost immediately after finishing his study of law, become a professional revolutionary.)

Together with the Marxian emigres around Plekhanov, who later became his most bitter enemy, Lenin, as co-editor of the *Iskra* (**Spark**) (1900-1903), fought all reformist or revisionist Russian socialists. Some of them, the Economists, dropped even their revolutionary aims and the fight for the conquest of political power, and became interested primarily in practical daily issues: the improvement of living conditions for the masses and better wages for the laboring man. In these polemics Lenin held that the workers by themselves would not be able to develop a truly revolutionary consciousness, and that this consciousness ought to be brought to them by the revolutionary intelligentsia. Lenin became convinced that a well-organized and disciplined revolutionary party was necessary to fight existing conditions.[40] Influenced by the writings of Tkachev,[41]

and perhaps by Netchayev, he stated the necessity for a strong conspiratorial leadership and criticized severely any dilettantism among
revolutionaries. Only if professional revolutionaries devoted their
whole lives to the fight against Tsarism, could they achieve the collapse of absolutist defenses, and only a careful organization could
secure and guarantee a continuity of the revolutionary movement.
This conception of the party as a kind of military organization, based
upon orthodox Marxian doctrine, as interpreted by Lenin (whose
views were regarded as *the* truth), resulted in a split between
Bolsheviks and Mensheviks at the London Social-Democratic Party
congress of 1903. Lenin was attacked by his adversaries as a dictator who would abolish all freedom of opinion in the party and
create a state of siege. But at this congress even Plekhanov, who
later fought Lenin and ended as an isolated representative of the
most moderate group of Russian socialists, (he died in 1918) remarked in his famous speech in London that the realization of
socialism may be achieved without democratic means.[42]

Lenin — the Head of a Sect

From 1903 to 1917 Lenin appeared to be only a more or less
isolated leader of a political sect which needed not to be taken too
seriously. His demand for an armed uprising did not play an important role during the revolution of 1905-1906; the uprising in
Moscow remained a local affair. Such men as Bogdanov, with
whom he cooperated for a time, were soon repudiated; he explained
all conflicts with his friends and followers in terms of their defection from true Marxism. Any interpretation of Marxism that
differed from his was denounced with the utmost bitterness. In
numerous conferences and congresses he continued his struggle with
the Mensheviks, who formed various groups in opposition to him.

Lenin fought those of his followers who refused to participate
in the elections for the Duma, the representative body granted by
the Tsar in 1905, or who demanded the recall of the elected deputies. He opposed the so-called liquidators who suggested the
liquidation of the outdated party, which was no longer adapted to

conditions under the semi-constitutional regime after 1905. He studied philosophical works in order to oppose those philosophical heretics who tried to combine Marxism with the doctrines of Mach and Avenarius or who, to his horror, wrote about the socialist movement as a new religion. He had to defend himself against the accusation that, despite the resolution of a party congress, he continued to use "expropriations," that is, armed robberies of money transports, and so on, to finance his group — the most famous of which, that of Tiflis, was organized with the help of Stalin.[43] These "expropriations" led to attacks on his "ethics." His opponents pointed out that he discredited the socialist movement by his tolerance of criminal elements.

After 1903 Lenin openly established a group of his own, though it was not until 1912 that the Bolsheviks officially established a separate organization. However, the factions of Bolsheviks and Mensheviks claimed even afterwards that they belonged to one party. It must be noted, too, that Lenin's organization was permeated, like all other revolutionary organizations, by spies.[44] Tchernomasov, the editor of the party paper, *Pravda,* was in the pay of the Tsarist police; another police agent, Malinovsky, succeeded in becoming a very close collaborator of Lenin and even a member of the Bolshevik Central Committee. It was such agents who aided in the last arrest (1913) of Stalin, who had joined the Bolsheviks as a young professional revolutionary organizer, although the majority of his Georgian socialist comrades accepted Menshevism.

But despite all these difficulties the Bolsheviks succeeded in gaining adherents among industrial workers, particularly in the Urals and in St. Petersburg. Though Lenin was then an emigré living abroad, he directed the work of the Bolshevik Duma deputies as well as of the editorial staff of *Pravda.* Different from other revolutionary intellectuals, Lenin was always aware of the conclusive importance of practical organizational work. For him the destruction of Tsarism was decisive; but this aim was hidden behind endless discussions, polemics, and quarrels. Lenin appeared to be a man who was absolutely intolerant, trying to impose his authority

by any means, and a fanatic for whom no moral restrictions existed
if his power and the influence of his party were at stake.

The Type of Professional Revolutionary

Along with the radical intellectuals, professional revolutionaries
became important in the Bolshevik party. It may even be said that
the history of the party can be characterized as a constant decrease
of the role played by the intellectuals, who loved discussions, and the
increase of the role of the revolutionaries, who loved clear, final
decisions and action. These professional revolutionaries simply
accepted the authority of Lenin and the party. They worked until
1917 in the underground as organizers, executing orders and minor
tasks, without much interest in the eternal discussions of the emigres.
Finally, under Stalin's leadership, they drove the intellectuals from
all positions of influence and took over power completely. Though
Lenin himself was an emigré, compelled to the busy production of
doctrinal decisions and to the demolition of his opponents in endless
polemics, he hated discussions without practical results. He tired of
listening to the uninterrupted talks of Martov, even before this
friend of his early years on the *Iskra* became, as one of the leading
Mensheviks, his political enemy. Thought and analysis (particularly
by writing programmatic resolutions) were for Lenin a means of
carrying out political actions.

But it must be emphasized that the type of professional revolutionary organizer for whom ideas and theories became schemes and
formulas, shared the basic attitude of the revolutionary intelligentsia. For these men the whole content and meaning of life was
reduced to political systems and political actions. This attitude
formed the basis of their cynical, ruthless conquest, maintenance,
and expansion of power.[45] They believed, as did the intellectuals,
that their political ideas were always right; that everything depended
upon the realization of their political creed; that all adversaries
were absolutely wrong and were, therefore, the most vicious, most
dangerous of men. Hence, the true revolutionaries had the right
and the obligation to use all possible means in order to destroy
them. But this destruction required power; before they had con-

quered power it was impossible to crush their adversaries, all those who became betrayers by deviating from "the absolute truth." Conflicts were affairs inside the organizations; it was obviously impossible for Lenin to order the liquidation of all representatives of reactionary Tsarism, liberal bourgeosie, and so on, or of those heretics who falsified Marxism.

But it is not by chance that almost all of the accusations made after 1917, following Lenin's seizure of power, were the same as those made before 1917. Lenin was denounced as an intolerant doctrinaire, mercilessly attacking all those who did not accept his interpretation of Marxism. Today, the Soviet leaders are criticized for the same self-righteous attitude, for their claim to infallibility, and their slander of all powers that do not submit to Soviet demands. It is pointed out that Lenin's belief that all means may be justifiably used for the benefit of the party is applied today, by the Soviet leaders, to increase their power. Lenin regulated all his relations with other men according to his evaluation of their usefulness for his party; similarly, for the Soviet Union the ally of today is the enemy of tomorrow, if considerations of power politics require such a change.

It was the combination of utopianism with self-righteous ruthlessness and cynical power politics that brought the founder of Bolshevism to power. Lenin's opponents, the leaders of the competing parties and groups, had too little practical understanding and too little brutality. They therefore did not dare to realize their utopian beliefs by exploiting the world around them, and by utilizing the naive expectations of others for their own seizure of power. They remained intellectuals, eternally discussing their programs and tactics. They avoided the responsibilities and the risks of power pretending that the hour for socialism had not yet arrived. The burden of government ought to be left to bourgeois groups; for Russia had first to pass through a capitalist stage in which the feudal-agrarian regime would be overcome. Lenin despised these talkers as weak men who lived to debate but were afraid to act. As such, they could be exploited for Bolshevik purposes and abandoned or destroyed later, after the Soviets had firmly established their own power.

It was because of Lenin's example that the Bolsheviks were the only revolutionary intellectuals who succeeded in making a ruthless activism the predominant attitude of their party. Lenin was at the same time an intellectual and a professional revolutionary organizer. He was a doctrinaire as well as a man of action. In this sense he could aver that he united theory and practice. The Bolshevik secular religion gave to him and to his party's action both unity and flexibility. He could claim to learn from the same revolution which he thought was accomplishing an objectively necessary development towards a utopian aim — the classless society, a society without coercion, a society of men with perfect social attitudes, able to organize and run a perfectly functioning life in which private and public interests would simply coincide.[46]

Lenin and World War I

Until 1917 Lenin himself seemed to be only an intolerant fanatic engaged in incessant polemics against those who did not accept his interpretation of Marxism and his political tactics.

After a brief stay in Russia during the Revolution of 1905 he lived abroad, but, although an emigré, he remained leader of the party. From Western Galicia, which at this time belonged to Austria, he determined the policies of the Bolshevik deputies in the Duma of 1912 and directed the editors of the Bolshevik party organ, *Pravda*. This behavior is typical of Bolshevism down to our time. Public representatives act as agents and mouthpieces of the party leadership (even when they apply the prescribed "general line" according to the circumstances). The instructions and orders from above remain final. After the outbreak of World War I Lenin moved into Switzerland. The leader of the Austrian Socialists, Victor Adler, obtained permission for him to leave Austria, whose police suspected this citizen of hostile Russia. From the beginning Lenin was uncompromisingly opposed to World War I. He regarded it as a fight between imperialists who utilized and slaughtered the masses for their egoistic purposes. He saw the war simply as a proof of the decomposition and decay of Capitalism and as a means of accelerating the Socialist world revolution. Therefore, he rejected most emphatically any patriotic attitude, any desire to defend one's own fatherland. He hoped for the defeat of reactionary Tsarism as well as of imperialist Germany and pseudo-democratic Western powers. He despised all Socialists who voted war credits and supported the war effort as characterless traitors who had gone over to the side of the imperialists. He did not accept such arguments as those advanced by the German Socialists who justified their backing of the imperial government after the outbreak of the war on the ground that ultra-reactionary Tsarism was *the* enemy, or those advanced by the French Socialists and by Plekhanov who held that the Germany of William II was an anti-democratic power. He became an enemy of Kautsky, the most influential theoretician of the German Socialists, who had not dared to advise against voting the war credits. Kautsky, whom Lenin had formerly admired, he now despised as a cowardly flunkey of Capitalism. Lenin was profoundly disappointed by the behavior of the German Social Democratic Party, which he had regarded as a model party. For weeks he was unable to believe that the German Socialists had supported the war, and discarded all such news as propagandistic lies.[47] This patriotism of the parties who had united in the Socialist Second International, founded in 1889, was proof to him that this supreme authority of international Socialism had disgraced itself and had completely collapsed.

While in Switzerland Lenin participated in the Socialist international conferences at Zimmerwald (1915) and Kienthal (1916).[48] These conferences were called by those socialists critical of the war-supporting attitude of their parties and leaders. The "patriotic" policies were criticized by the majority at Zimmerwald and Kienthal on pacifistic and humanitarian grounds. Lenin belonged to a minority in Zimmerwald and Kienthal; he was not a pacifist like the majority, for he believed it necessary to use any means to transform the imperialist war into a revolutionary war for the victory of Socialism. While waiting for this change he wrote his book on *Imperialism,* employing cautious and veiled language; it was to be published in Tsarist Russia. His influence in Russia during the war years was limited; he had very little communication with the country of his birth. The attitude of the Bolshevik Duma deputies, who together with their adviser Kamenev were tried in 1915 before a court, disappointed him — they did not come out energetically enough against the war.

The war years were years of isolation for Lenin. He was separated from his future collaborator, Stalin, whom he had met briefly at party conferences and during a longer stay in Austria; from 1913 the future master of the Soviet Union was exiled in Siberia, and this time he did not escape from his place of banishment, as he had several times before. Lenin continued to disagree with Trotsky, who, at the congress of 1903, had supported his enemies.[49] Bitter polemics developed also with Piatakov and Bukharin who did not approve Lenin's view that it was right for national groups to secede from the state under whose domination they had lived; according to them nationalist demands would not matter for the socialist party. It is quite understandable that under these conditions Lenin suffered from fits of despair. A few weeks before Tsarism collapsed in March 1917 he stated that he had no chance of returning during his lifetime to Russia, for he would not see the day of the successful revolution.

For, despite his belief in the coming anti-imperialist revolution, Lenin did not at all expect that the year 1917 would see the disappearance of the Tsarist regime as well as the rise of his Bolshevik party from a little-known sect of Russian Socialism to a group dominating Russia — and even more, to a movement threatening mankind with revolution. How did this surprising development come about? The collapse of Tsarism was surely not the result of Bolshevik propaganda and activity. The small Bolshevik organization of Petrograd, led by young Molotov, did not play any role in the disorders and street fights resulting in the seizure of power by a Provisional Government. This government had a dual basis: on the one side, it grew out of a Duma committee under the leadership of such liberals as Miliukov; and, on the other, it was approved by a Soviet (Council of Workers) composed of moderate Socialists. Nor did the Bolsheviks play a great role, even after Stalin's return from his Siberian exile. They continued to form a group opposing the provisional government without much energy and influence.

Conquest of Power

After he heard about the end of Tsarism, Lenin developed his program: "All power to the Soviets"— which, of course, he believed would be dominated by his party — and no confidence in the imperialist-capitalist Provisional Government. Lenin succeeded, despite all the difficulties created by the Allies, in returning to Russia; along with other radical socialists he obtained permission from Imperial Germany to cross her territory. Lenin and the Russian socialists such as the Menshevik Martov, who opposed the war, were regarded by the German General Staff as useful instruments with which to undermine the Russian army.[50] After his arrival in the Russian capital Lenin imposed his program, the so-called April theses, on the Bolshevik party. Stalin himself has confessed that he saw the light only after the issuance of these theses.[51] Under Lenin's leadership the Bolshevik party exploited the rising anarchial moods of the masses.[52] As the soldiers became more and more tired of war, the Bolshevik propaganda against the imperialist war became increasingly successful among them. They refused to take orders from their officers; they preferred their pleasant, comfortable, and secure stay in Petrograd to risking their lives at the front. For the workers and peasants Revolution meant a change in property conditions. The peasants became unwilling to postpone the demand for a radical agrarian reform until a national constitutional assembly was elected and convened. This was not scheduled to occur until after the war. Therefore the masses were impressed by the Bolshevik slogan: loot what has been looted! Democratic liberties like the freedom of press and assembly introduced by the provisional government did not impress the masses — they wanted the land of big

37

estate owners to be distributed among them. Also national groups — like the Ukrainians — were dissatisfied with the Provisional Government's attempt to maintain centralism, despite a few concessions to federalist views; they regarded this policy as aiming at the maintenance of domination by the Great Russians.[53] Furthermore, the moderate socialist parties, then in control of the Soviets, were quarrelling among themselves and had little trust in the provisional government; they organized demonstrations in May 1917 which forced the abdication of Foreign Minister Miliukov who had developed an annexationist program. (He was called in the Bolshevik propaganda Miliukov Dardanelski because in 1917 he put forward demands for the control of the Dardanelles similar to those made by Stalin's Soviet government after World War II.)

The Provisional Government was very weak. A constant reshuffling took place. The situation did not improve even after Kerensky, the moderate agrarian socialist, replaced the weak liberal Lwow as prime minister, and after leaders of moderate socialist groups such as the Menshevik Tseretelli and the Socialist Revolutionary Tchernov joined the Cabinet. The dissolution of the army was hastened by the unsuccessful attempt to start an offensive in Galicia.

True, a first attempt of the Bolsheviks to come to power in July 1917 by means of street demonstrations in Petrograd failed. Lenin went into hiding. Trotsky, who had joined Lenin's party, was arrested. In August, General Kornilov, the commander-in-chief of the army, tried to put an end to anarchy by moving troops against Petrograd. He intended to form a national government and offered Kerensky a post.[54] But this attempt failed completely. Kerensky opposed it, and radical workers were given arms by the defenders of the Provisional Government; the Bolsheviks were also used to defeat the threat by Kornilov. The control of the Soviets in Moscow and Petrograd shifted now from the moderate socialists to the Bolsheviks. Trotsky, released from prison, obtained the key position as chairman of the Soviet in Petrograd. Kerensky and his Provisional Government, despite their apparent victory over the military putsch, lost all authority. They tried vainly to regain it by organizing bodies of representatives appointed by the several parties and social groups.

During these weeks Lenin appealed incessantly to the central committee of his party to take over power by force.[55]   The Bolshevik party leadership hesitated; Zinoviev and Kamenev, two particularly close collaborators of Lenin, publicly protested against the planned seizure of power. Finally, the Bolshevik overthrow of the Provisional Government was scheduled by the Central Committee to coincide with the opening of the Second Russian Soviet Congress. So anarchic were the prevailing conditions that the October revolution, which ended Kerensky's rule and opened the Soviet regime, was accomplished by comparatively small armed groups: only a batallion of women was willing to defend the Winter Palace, the seat of the Provisional Government.   The majority of the Soviet Congress acclaimed the new cabinet, which was named the Council of People's Commissars. Lenin was the chairman; Trotsky took over the commissariat of foreign affairs and Stalin of nationalities. An attempt by Kerensky to reconquer Petrograd failed miserably; the Cossacks, led by the ultra-conservative General Krasnov, were considering his extradition to the Bolsheviks just as he fled. Resistance against the new regime was only sporadic; it was most serious in Moscow.

Tactics After the Seizure of Power

Lenin came to power, first, because he had made his party into a disciplined and comparatively well-organized group; secondly, because the other parties — particularly the agrarian socialists, the so-called Socialist Revolutionaries, who had more followers than the Bolsheviks — had no strong leaders and no concrete practical program; and thirdly, because Lenin and his collaborators succeeded by propaganda and other tactics in giving the impression that they would achieve the wishes of the masses. The peasants, for example, were satisfied by a decree giving them practically all the land of the estate owners.[56]   The enemies of Lenin's regime, and therefore of the land decree, were suspected of willingness to restore the hated

39

property distribution of the past. It did not matter that Lenin and the Bolsheviks were (correctly) accused of copying their land decree from the un-Marxian socialist-revolutionaries. This fact proves that from the beginning of their rule the Bolsheviks subordinated doctrinal claims to power considerations. They believed that the over-all development would justify the doctrine, but that the methods to be used in a particular moment had to be adapted to experience. When, in November 1917, Lenin published his book on *State and Revolution,* he wrote in a postscript that it is much more important to participate in the Revolution, that is, to learn from practical experience, than to write about it or merely to develop theories.

The longing of the masses for an end to the war was satisfied by an appeal to all belligerents to start armistice negotiations. This appeal was not accepted by the Allies, but it did lead to an armistice with Germany. The result of peace negotiations with the Central Powers was the Treaty of Brest-Litovsk. This separate peace was very unfavorable for Russia.[57] She lost all the territories occupied by Germany and her allies; the Ukraine became a nominally independent state under German occupation. A civil war in Finland ended, with German aid, in a victory for the white anti-Red forces.

Lenin had great difficulty in persuading his party to accept the treaty with the Central Powers.[58] He warned that the Germans, if their conditions were not accepted, would simply order their armies to march into Russia and end the Soviet regime. Lenin's assertion proved to be correct. For, after Trotsky, the chief of the Soviet delegation, refused to accept the German proposals and broke off negotiations, declaring that there would be neither peace nor war, the German military forces did advance against Russia. The final conditions, which the Soviets had to accept in order to survive, were harder than those offered to Trotsky. Lenin's fight for the acceptance of the peace of Brest-Litovsk by the ruling party is a classic example of the typical Bolshevist combination of doctrinaire utopianism and flexible power politics. Lenin insisted that revolutionary propaganda leaflets could not stop Russia's enemies; in his polemics against the left-Communists under Bukharin, Radek, and others, who had formed a faction opposing him, he pointed out that it is the duty of genuine revolutionaries to take into consideration existing power conditions and not to fall victim to high-sounding pseudo-revolutionary rhetoric: a temporary retreat may be necessary in order to make possible a new advance in the future.[59] Such an advance could take place when the collapse of Imperial Germany in November 1918 made the annulment of the treaty of Brest-Litovsk possible.

The first months of the regime were notably influenced by propagandistic considerations. It was necessary through a radical break with the past to prove the revolutionary character of the Soviet regime. Reactionary institutions were abolished by decrees; they were designed to show that the socialist government could accomplish quickly an antifeudal revolution which the bourgeoisie alone could only have accomplished much more slowly, if at all. The break-up of the old army and bureaucracy was facilitated through a strike started by civil servants who believed that the new regime was illegal because it was created by the use of force. A separation between Church and State was introduced with the intent of weakening religious groups, particularly the Orthodox Church, which had been accustomed to support by public authorities. The constitutional-democratic party (Cadets) of Miliukov was outlawed as counterrevolutionary. The Che-Ka, the extraordinary commission, invested with unlimited power, was created to fight counterrevolution, speculation, and sabotage, with the firm help and participation of Lenin, who emphasized that it was necessary for the dictatorship of the proletariat to use force and violence.[60] The seizure of the larger bank accounts and the opening of bank deposit boxes was intended to prove the anticapitalist character of the Soviet rule.

The basic democratic practice of free elections, whereby majorities could change, was abandoned. The national constitutional assembly was closed down in January, 1918, after its first session and was not permitted to meet again,[61] because the elections which

41

had occurred shortly before and after the October revolution had provided a non-Bolshevik majority. The Bolsheviks could not control the assembly, even with the co-operation of the left Socialist-Revolutionaries who, at that time, supported Lenin's government. Therefore, they claimed that the composition of the assembly did not correspond to the true will of the people, which was presumed to support the regime established by the October revolution. This attitude was no surprise; Lenin had warned repeatedly against constitutional illusions and had written in October to the Central Committee of his party: "It is naive to wait for a formal majority for the Bolsheviks. No revolution does that." [62]

At the beginning, the Soviet regime was based on a coalition of the Bolsheviks and the left Socialist-Revolutionaries who supposedly represented the peasants. But the left Socialist-Revolutionaries did not play a great or even a substantial role. They refused to accept the treaty of Brest-Litovsk and left the government. In July, 1918, after a putsch more sensational than dangerous, they vanished into the world of illegality. Though a Menshevik group which supported the Soviet government in a fight against White Russian groups was disbanded as late as 1921, it can be said that Lenin's regime was from its inauguration a one-party regime — a fact which has remained unchanged despite all the other changes and shifts which have occurred since the October revolution. Of course, Lenin's Communist Party of 1917-1918 permitted free discussions and even forgave public opposition to the party leadership, but the development of the party into its present form in which all such freedom is crushed was the consequence of Lenin's principles and attitudes.

The Development of the Soviet Regime

a) 1917-1921: War Communism and NEP

A brief survey of the various phases of the Soviet regime will give a general picture of its development. In the first months of propaganda decrees and the destruction of traditional groups and institutions, Lenin began to change from a negative policy of destroying the old regime and its heritage to a policy of building up the instruments of power for the new regime. His acceptance of the peace treaty of Brest-Litovsk and his emphasis upon order and discipline prove that Lenin realized the necessity of taking existing conditions into account. There was some hesitation before socialization of industrial enterprises occurred;[63] for Lenin and the party had believed that it would be sufficient for the workers to control and direct the bourgeois capitalists. But this control proved unworkable and the regime was forced to seize the enterprises.

However, even Lenin himself, despite his basic realism, sometimes inclined toward utopian projects, such as that aiming at a quick transformation of society with the help of a universal labor service and the abolition of money payment.[64] At the same time, he realized the necessity for educating the masses as well as the representatives of the new regime. The role of non-Bolshevik specialists was stressed, as was the necessity for learning from the technical experiences of the past.

The first period, which combined utopian experiments and decrees with attempts at a realistic approach, prepared the organization of a strong political power and the imposition of discipline on the masses; soon it developed into the period of civil war and so-called War Communism (1918-1920). During this second period Communist policy was dominated by the need to crush the various White armies.[65] These armies received support, first from some German military circles, who in 1918 opposed the policy of the German Foreign Office and aided the efforts to destroy the revolutionary Red regime. After the disappearance of Imperial Germany, the Allies aided the White Russian armies. Despite the collapse of the original hopes that the confiscatory policies of this period would achieve the quick construction of a socialist-communist society, these policies did make it possible for the Communists to conduct and win the civil war. For, though production had decreased to a minimum, confiscation proved a sufficient means of obtaining supplies for the Red army.

The defeat in the war against Poland (1920), the well-known

uprising in Kronstadt (the naval port of Petrograd), and the lesser known peasants' revolts in Central Russia, caused Lenin to call for a retreat after the Red victory in the civil war. The White armies had suffered annihilating defeats; they had been unable to co-ordinate their operations because they were weakened by conflicts between democratic and moderate-socialistic politicians on the one side, and the conservative military leadership on the other; they did not receive, despite many promises, enough support from abroad; and they often incensed the masses of the people — workers in industrial areas and peasants, particularly in Siberia — by seeming to favor the return to an outdated prerevolutionary social order.

On the other hand, Lenin realized that the exhausted and tired masses needed a return to normal conditions after their sacrifices and sufferings during the civil war. He realized, too, that a quick transformation of World War I into a world revolution would not take place. The collapse of Imperial Germany and of the Hapsburg Dual Monarchy did not result in the rise of Communist regimes; the Soviet regimes in Bavaria and Hungary were of brief duration. The Soviets were unable to reconquer the Baltic States and to impose a Communist government upon Poland, though they did succeed in establishing a Ukrainian Soviet Republic and, later, in conquering the Menshevik Republic of Georgia.

Lenin's foreign policy, like his domestic policy, had a dual character from the beginning. The Third International, founded in Moscow in 1919, aimed to prepare and organize revolution outside Russia by unifying the various pro-Communist groups and directing the development of the various Communist parties.[66] The Comintern imposed 21 points upon parties wishing to join; it kept authority in its own hands and excluded socialist leaders it regarded as untrustworthy. But at the same time treaties were concluded by the Soviet regime with capitalist governments, the independence of the Baltic States was recognized, for the Soviet government realized that its attempt to impose communist government upon these states, after the German collapse of 1918, had failed. Poland received territorial concessions by the treaty of Riga, after the Soviet armies were routed at Warsaw. The treaty of Rapallo established friendly relations with Germany and permitted the utilization of German military experience by the Red Army. The treaty was concluded in 1922 with the Weimar Republic,[67] though this regime had originated from a defeat imposed upon German pro-Communists. The realistic policy of Rapallo did not end revolutionary expectations and policies; the Soviet leaders tried — though without success — to establish Communist domination in Germany, while the Weimar Republic was weakened by the Ruhr conflict of 1923. This realistic foreign policy, however, was based not only upon calculations of Russian national interest, but also took into consideration the limits of Soviet strength as well as the decline of revolutionary enthusiasm and fluidity in the world after 1920. However, despite their realism, Soviet leaders did not give up hope for a world revolution in the long run.

They simply shifted their emphasis from the aim of rapid world revolution starting in Western countries to the aim of increasing and enhancing the power of the existing Soviet regime. During the Brest-Litovsk crisis Lenin stressed the importance of the fact that the Soviet regime was in being — the healthy first-born child of the world revolution. Work for the world revolution became more and more identified with a foreign policy that guaranteed the security of the Soviet Union and strengthened its power. This foreign policy with its maneuvers and shifts was the product of the delay in the coming of the world revolution. While waiting for this revolution the Soviet regime had to be strengthened; it had to learn from the experiences and technical achievements of other powers and nations. As Lenin has put it: "We must utilize Capitalism in order to build Socialism." Soviet leaders recognized the usefulness of economic relations with capitalist states just as they accepted as a fact the power of Imperial Germany in the Brest-Litovsk period. The Soviet leaders recognized the temporary necessity for the co-existence of the Soviet and the capitalist world; they expected that as the Soviet world would progress and grow stronger, the capitalist world would decay and grow weaker. The weak links

45

in the capitalistic chain should be discovered. Lenin's analysis of Imperialism overcame the traditional Marxian belief that the revolution must result from a prior development of Capitalism to maturity in the industrialized countries with a strong proletariat. According to Lenin, the revolution could be brought about in colonial, exploited regions which were trying at the same time to accomplish a bourgeois-nationalist liberation. The doctrinaire utopianism of Bolshevism did not exclude shifting power politics; on the contrary, it imposed them. The Bolshevik regime had to maneuver in order to survive until proper conditions — namely, its own strength and the weakness of the other powers — would permit a new advance.

b)   1921-1927: Stalin's Rise to Power

The whole period of 1921-1927 can be characterized as a period in which the Soviet regime tried to gain strength for such a new advance. This period opened with Lenin's introduction of the New Economic Policy (NEP), designed to make concessions to the tired and exhausted masses. A limited free market and private trade were admitted in the interest of the peasants. Lenin even offered "concessions" to foreign capitalists in order to make investments in Soviet Russia attractive to them — a policy which did not have the success expected. Principles of calculation and the stringencies of legalistic rules were emphasized and introduced, replacing the former policies of confiscation without regulations, which had aided in winning the civil war. But the "commanding positions" remained in the hands of the party. The nationalized economy controlled the sector into which private initiative was admitted. Banks, big enterprises, and foreign trade remained under the control of the Soviet state. No other parties were permitted alongside the Bolshevik party. A committee which was organized in the hunger-catastrophe of 1922 was dissolved when its non-Bolshevik members tried to gain independent influence. The Che-Ka was rechristened G-P-U; but even under formal legal supervision, it retained its basically unlimited powers. The consolidation of the regime advanced.

The loose confederation of Soviet Republics — of which the

Russian and Ukrainian were the most important ones — was held together by the solidarity and unity of the Communists; it was replaced in 1922 by the Soviet Union. The USSR was nominally a federation, but in reality, despite the explicit statement of its constitution about the right of secession, it continued to concentrate power in Moscow. True, this tendency towards centralization was camouflaged by a policy which opposed the remnants of Tsarist Great Russian chauvinism. In the Ukrainian Soviet Republic a policy of Ukrainization was favored. Former Ukrainian nationalist leaders, like the historian Hrushevsky, were permitted to participate in public life. But also in the period of apparent concessions to non-Russian nationalism the authority of the leadership in the party was strengthened. The tenth party congress, on Lenin's initiative, forbade factional groupings inside the party.[69] Lenin had tired of opposition groups, like the so-called worker opposition, which protested against increasing bureaucratization of the party and of public life. But Lenin could afford some controversial discussions inside the party. His authority had become so undisputed that he could successfully utilize at the same time men like Stalin and Trotsky even though they were estranged by their bitter quarrels during the civil war.

During Lenin's illness (he was incapacitated in 1922 and died in 1924), an internal struggle about who was to succeed him developed within the party leadership. Upon Zinoviev's suggestion Stalin had been made secretary general of the party in 1922. He used this office to bring the party machine, step by step, under his control. Together with Kamenev and Zinoviev, two typical Bolshevik intellectuals, he prevented Trotsky from becoming Lenin's heir and helped reduce his influence in the party. Then Stalin turned against his allies of the first hour and in their turn deprived them of power. Now they joined with Trotsky, opposing Stalin in a bloc. But it was too late. Stalin could use the party machine against the opposition; the party voted always in Stalin's favor and did not listen to the arguments of the opposition. Of course, all competitors in the fight for power cited Lenin as the highest infallible authority. Zinoviev had coined the expression "Leninism"

47

and had tried to discredit Trotsky by utilizing Lenin's old polemics against him. It is remarkable that Stalin moved very cautiously during this time and disallowed "bloodletting in the Party." [70] He refused to sacrifice the rightist Bukharin to Zinoviev, who demanded his head. In 1927 the opposition was expelled from the party; its leaders submitted more or less eagerly to the official line; and Trotsky was exiled (1929) from the Soviet Union.

c) 1927-1936: Totalitarian Planning and the Stalin Constitution

The Bolsheviks under Stalin organized and consolidated their complete control of the Soviet Union according to a definite totalitarian pattern. The Five Year plans for the organization of production and the acceleration of industrialization were put into operation. After 1929, Stalin, against the opposition of rightists Tomsky, Bukharin, and Rykov, carried out the collectivization of agriculture from above, using every form of compulsion.[71] For millions of people, this policy resulted in death through hunger, or in deportation to labor camps.[72] For Stalin was determined to destroy the independence of the peasants who had threatened the process of industrialization by their refusal to supply cities with foodstuffs. The peasants were forced into kolhozes controlled by party officials and had to fulfill production quotas imposed from above. They were forced to adopt agricultural machinery in order to form a market for the products of the industrial plants; the government organized and controlled the centers (stations) for the machines.

The millions deported as forced labor brought a change in the activities of the GPU.[73] Its concentration camps had served to isolate active or potential enemies of the regime; now these camps became enterprises for economic and colonizing purposes. The Volga-White Sea canal had served as a preparatory experiment for the exploitation of forced labor; now deportees, political and criminal prisoners, could be used on a much larger scale in the almost unpopulated regions of Northern Europe as well as of Asiatic Russia. In other words, terror was now combined with economic planning. The chance to become members of the camp's admin-

48

istrative as well as directing group, and the carefully planned proportion between the amount of work performed and the amount of food given were destined to increase the productivity of forced labor. The official propaganda, of course, presented the camps and the regions of exile as places where antisocial persons could be rehabilitated and transformed into socially useful persons and valuable members of the socialist community.

During this period when the U.S.S.R. became definitely organized as a totalitarian state, foreign policy was, until 1933, dominated by the fear that the Western powers might again intervene against the Soviet regime as they did after World War I. The U.S.S.R. denounced the League of Nations, to which it did not belong, as a hypocritical pseudo-moral institution organized in order to prepare and justify such an intervention. The Soviet Union co-operated with Germany for economic reasons as well as to prevent united action by a united capitalist front. The treaty of Rapallo developed into the treaty of Berlin in 1926. The Comintern through its lack of success lost its prestige and independence, and became more and more clearly an instrument of Soviet foreign policy. This was confirmed by Trotsky's attempts to use it as a weapon against Stalin's policy — they failed completely. More and more emphasis was put on relations with China, and the U.S.S.R. made a great impression on the Chinese when it abandoned the unequal treaties and privileges Russia had received from them. The Soviets also supported the Chinse movement for national liberation, though their hopes to co-operate with the Kuomintang failed after the death of Sun Yat Sen (the founder of the Chinese Republic), because Chiang Kai-shek broke with Moscow. But a Communist party was permanently established in China. It accepted the basic tenets of Leninism, although it tried to utilize specific features of the agrarian crisis in China in order to seize power.[74] Having regained the Russian Asiatic territories, lost in the first years after the establishment of the Soviet regime, the Soviet Union adopted a very cautious policy toward Japan, giving up its privileges in Manchuria — the Soviet leaders were anxious to avoid an open external conflict.

49

A new period of Soviet foreign policy started in 1934 when Hitler's Nazi regime became definitely established in Germany. Fearing a Nazi crusade, the Soviet Union turned to the West. A military alliance with France was concluded; membership in the League of Nations was asked for and received; diplomatic recognition by the United States at the end of 1933 was highly appreciated. These policies gave rise to the belief that the Soviet Union was on the way to democratization. This belief was also encouraged by the preparation and acceptance of the Stalin Constitution (1936). This document not only omitted revolutionary statements but granted equal rights to all Soviet citizens; whereas previously certain groups — for example Tsarist officials and priests — were deprived of such rights or franchise. The new appreciation of Russia's past (demonstrated by the condemnation of the late historian, Pokrovsky, who stressed the role of commercial capitalism in Russian history and denounced the sins of the Tsarist regime),[75] also strengthened the erroneous opinion of many, that the Soviet Union had abandoned, under Stalin's leadership, its world revolutionary designs. It was believed that Stalin was exclusively interested in a powerful Russian state. Had not Stalin emphasized, from the beginning of his fight with Trotsky, the necessity of building up socialism in one country, whereas his adversary upheld the necessity of "permanent revolution," believing that uprisings abroad were required for the existence of the Soviet regime?

d)   1936-1939: The Great Purge and the Turn to Hitler's Germany

Those who believed the Soviet Union was on its way to democracy regarded the collectivization of agriculture as the last application of mass terror. But the hope that the Soviet Union was on the road to democracy was soon shaken. In 1936, even before the Stalin Constitution was put into force, the purges were inaugurated, directed against old Bolsheviks, distinguished party members, officials, and generals.[76] Potential as well as actual enemies of Stalin's regime became the victims. Close friends of Lenin, like Kamenev and Zinoviev, made startling public confessions and were sentenced

50

to death. The execution of other leading Bolsheviks, like Karakhan and Enukidse, was made known by brief notices; leading military men, such as Marshall Tukhatchevsky and General Yakir, were executed after secret trials; others, like Marshals Jegorov and Bluecher, simply disappeared. Jagoda, who for many years had been the head of the political police and had prepared the first great trial of the purge, admitted abjectly and publicly the most heinous crimes; the peak of this period was named 'Ezhovschina' after Jagoda's successor, Ezhov, who ruthlessly performed countless liquidations and arrests until he, too, finally vanished from public life.

The great purge from 1936 to 1938 definitely established Stalin's absolute control over the Party. Those Communists who had known and opposed him as one of Lenin's lieutenants disappeared. Intellectuals like the former emigres, inclined to discussion and skepticism, were now replaced by "apparatchiki" (men of the apparatus) who carried out orders without any hesitation. Party doctrine for them consisted in formulas applied in accordance with the interpretation and meaning determined by the highest authorities.

The great purge stabilized definitively a totalitarian rule by an omnipotent Soviet leadership. Perpetuating itself by controlling everything with the help of a subservient bureaucracy, it pretended (and still pretends) to fulfill and interpret authoritatively an absolutely true doctrine. But, as we have seen, this development was not a break with Lenin's principles; Stalin's extension of terroristic methods to the party was only an application of these principles. Stalin had instruments for establishing the regime which Lenin, fighting for a conquest of power, obviously did not yet have. Stalin had an additional motive for using these instruments, for despite all the adulation bestowed upon him after 1929, he did not have the unquestioned authority in the party enjoyed by Lenin. Stalin realized after the assassination of his lieutenant Kirov that the opposition against him in the party had only been driven underground, and that continued terror would be required to make his position secure.

Soviet foreign policy was, on the whole, rather on the defensive from the end of the civil war until Hitler's rise to power in 1933. The danger of an attack by Nazi Germany was countered by a shift in Soviet foreign policy. The friendly relations established with Western powers and the membership in the League of Nations (1934) were attempts to win support for the Soviet Union against Nazi Germany.[77] The cooperation of communists with moderate socialists in so-called popular fronts was undertaken for the same purpose, although the latter had been formerly denounced as the worst traitors and as "social fascists."

e)   1939-1945: Soviet Policies During World War II

But the turn to the West was discouraged by the Munich conference of 1938, to which the U.S.S.R. was not invited. The West, led by Chamberlain, the prime minister of appeasement, made concessions to Hitler. Therefore, in the spring of 1939 Litvinov, the foreign commissar, who was the symbol of anti-Nazi western orientation, was dismissed. From August 1939, by means of the nonaggression pact negotiated by Litvinov's successor, Molotov, and Hitler's foreign minister, Ribbentrop, the Soviet Union tried to exploit Hitler's aggression for its own security and benefit, opening the gate for German aggression against Poland, which caused World War II.[78] This pact promised Soviet neutrality in the case of German aggression, and accordingly assured the Nazis of no involvement in a dangerous two-front war. In a secret annex the pact provided that, if Germany expanded to the East, the Soviet Union would be compensated by the partition of Poland; the whole of Eastern Europe was divided into spheres of interest.

What had been obvious for years in Soviet internal policies was now confirmed by the Union's foreign policy. What really mattered was the preservation and the expansion of the power of the totalitarian state; the existence and constant strengthening of this state were seen by the Soviet leaders as the best instrument and the safest guarantee for the coming victory of socialism and communism everywhere in the world. The communist attempts to conquer power by internal revolutions had failed outside the U.S.S.R., regardless of the activities of the Third International. In the U.S.S.R., on the contrary, power had not only been achieved but stabilized and expanded. Therefore, the Soviet party and the Soviet Union became exemplary in all respects; everything serving its existence and strength was good. The Leninist political religion had created and justified the totalitarian state (the dictatorship of the proletariat represented by the party), and this totalitarian state had developed from a means to an end in the present era.

The victory of socialism and the communist party had been accomplished in the U.S.S.R. and was accompanied by a surge of Soviet nationalism — its victories and grand purpose entitled the U.S.S.R. to universal leadership and to unlimited self-glorification.[79]

In 1941 Hitler's attack forced the Soviet Union to fight on the side of the Allies. The war was conducted as a great patriotic war; and the dissolution of the Third International in 1943 seemed to confirm the end of Soviet interest in world revolution. But as soon as the military defeat of the Nazis appeared certain, Soviet power politics came again into the open. These tactics were warranted not so much by the claim that they served the coming communist classless society as by the assertion that they were the necessary means of protecting the Soviet Union against hostile actions and menacing interventions by the Western powers, particularly the United States, the leading imperialist power. Soviet expansionism was favored by the general situation at the end of World War II. Soviet control of Central Europe and the Balkans as well as the extraordinary prestige of Soviet military power were advantageous for the domination of the Soviet Union on the one hand; on the other hand they increased fear of threatening world revolution. Their basic doctrinal approach made the Soviet leaders regard the world as necessarily split into two camps. They believe that one of these camps, the capitalist-imperialist one, of course, must collapse in the end, though only after a long and protracted struggle.

f)   Since 1945: The Cold War

Soviet expansionism led to the cold war with the United States and the West. The capitalist Allies of World War II inherited the role of Hitler as the main enemy of the socialist world. The revolutionary situations created by the war had to be exploited. The Soviet Union expanded and organized its power by establishing its system of satellites, by encouraging the victory of the communist party in China, by harrassing the imperialistic world with attacks and local wars such as that in Korea, and by intensifying and exploiting all conflicts such as those precipitated by the rise of Asiatic and Mid-Eastern nationalisms against colonial powers.

The circle is closed — the world revolution is now a function of Soviet expansionist foreign policy and the successes of Soviet foreign policy serve the world revolution. In Europe the Soviet-controlled satellite states increase the power of the U.S.S.R.; and in Asia the Soviet-supported Chinese communist party wins the civil war. A few defeats are suffered, of course: Marshal Tito of Yugoslavia breaks away from Soviet control; the policies of expansionism and non-cooperation result in reactions. The Truman doctrine is directed against further Soviet expansion and is implemented economically by the Marshall Plan and militarily by the Atlantic Pact. The attempt of the North Korean satellite to take over South Korea permits the United Nations (under the leadership of the United States) to prove that new attempts at expansion will be met with armed resistance. Despite endless declarations that it is for peace and disarmament whereas the United States and the Atlantic powers are for aggression and armament, the Soviet Union continues to lose influence over world public opinion as well as over the international labor movement. But the Stalinist policy emphasizes the power of the Soviet Union, and its military might continues to inspire fear in spite of all military and political counter-measures involved in the so-called policy of containment.[80]

The Soviet Union expects in the long run to win the cold war without risking a shooting war on a global scale. Soviet exploitation of conflicts among other powers and the burdens of the armament race will assure and intensify world-wide social and political crises. Internal conflicts in the capitalist camp will compensate for Soviet technical and economic inferiority.

Since World War II the internal policies of the Soviet Union have been designed to continue and to augment absolute control by Stalinist leadership. The role of the party is again stressed — the party under Stalin's direction has won the war — whereas the role of the generals is played down. The emphasis upon the "hegemonial people" (Stalin), that is, the Great Russians, serves to focus the power of the regime and present it as a universal model to be imitated everywhere. The disappearance of the Comintern — only partially replaced by the Cominform — indicates that the Soviet Union possesses directly and immediately the leadership of the Communist movement in the world.[81] The doctrinal claim to dominate and define all fields is now systematically exercized in such vastly different fields as literature, philosophy, music, botany, and philology, where the party directives and orders must be accepted.[82] Unreliable elements are purged, often after the most humiliating public confessions. Confidence in the achievements of the Soviet regime is also expressed in the fight against cosmopolitanism and all foreign influences. The Soviet regime does not need any outside help. Created by the Russian people, it manifests the superiority of the Russian people, whose creativity and inventiveness are signposts to the whole world. The fact that Bolshevism-Communism succeeded in getting and maintaining power in Russia is responsible for the nationalization of the doctrine. Bolshevism assumes increasingly today the features of intense Russian nationalism.

The Totalitarian State

The Bolshevik regime construes itself to have started as a dictatorship founded upon an alliance between the proletariat and the poor peasants.[83] It pretends to have been an alliance in which the proletariat is the leading group, with policies determined by its avant-garde, the disciplined, well-organized "monolithic" Bolshevik party. Today the official doctrine explains that socialism is realized in the Soviet Union: the economy is entirely socialized; private ownership of the means of production (and therefore the division of society into classes) has been abolished; all-out planning, extending to agriculture, has been introduced. True, a Communism in which everybody will be rewarded according to his needs, has not yet been achieved. In the present phase the principle prevails that rewards are differentiated according to the individual's contribution to society.[84] But the Soviet regime is proud to have achieved socialism at a time when the western moderate socialists have merely become tools of capitalism, members of coalition cabinets, and union leaders are helping, despite their social reforms and policies, to maintain the bourgeois world. Lenin had written after the outbreak of World War I that the Great Russian proletariat could develop a national pride on the basis of the Russian, anti-Tsarist revolutionary movement; the Soviet leaders of today justify their nationalism by the successful realization of socialism in the U.S.S.R.

Contrary to Lenin's original expectations and announcements, formulated particularly in his *State and Revolution* (1917), the alleged realization of socialism was not accompanied by a corresponding withering away of the state (the instrument of coercion in the interest of one class). Lenin had hoped that with the advance of the dictatorship of the proletariat, the organs of the state separated from the people, like the army and the bureaucracy, would disappear. All these announcements, expectations and hopes have not come true. In the current reinterpretation of Lenin by Stalin,[85] it is maintained that during the present epoch, with imperialistic powers surrounding the Soviet Union, the state and its power machinery are required to protect (and to expand) socialist society. Stalin emphasizes the necessity for the state's continuing existence even after the realization of socialism in the Soviet Union. This acceptance of the state as official doctrine has increased tremendously the employment of power and violence. Pressure is applied in order to accomplish the transformation of society and the education of the masses; the doctrine of the necessary development of society towards the aims of socialism and communism justifies this systematic, ruthlessly cool pressure. Terrorism is unavoidable in order to force the masses in the right direction. Here Bolshevist policies rejoin typical traditions of Russian Muscovite history where brutal power is applied from above to shape society (Ivan the Terrible, Peter the Great). Industrial backwardness must be overcome by promoting an artificial acceleration of economic developments through constant compulsion from above, disregarding, as the forced collectivization of agriculture and the large masses in the labor camps show, the will and welfare of the people and society.

On the other hand, a minimum of legal security is necessary, without which neither administration nor economic planning could function. Therefore, the policies of the Bolshevik regime are dominated by the endeavor to combine the two contradictory elements of terrorism and legal security.[86] Terrorism is necessary as a demonstration of the limitless power of the rulers responsible for the realization of an absolutely true doctrine, for terrorism is the expression of a power which is not limited by law. This very power shows that the purposes of the regime determine the contents and interpretation of the law. Concern for the endurance of Communist rule supersedes, for example, all guarantees of individual rights in the Stalin Constitution, so that even leading Communists have been mercilessly purged (often without any court procedure by administrative justice of the Secret Police) despite the provisions of the Constitution and of the party rules. Yet the necessity for a strictly legalistic attitude is emphasized; laws and rules must be observed, for without such observance the political-social system could not function. Therefore, periods of terrorism like that of the forced collectivization of agriculture or of the great purge of 1936-1938 are followed by periods of legalism and stabilization. After Ezhov had destroyed by his mass arrests and executions any feeling of security among members of the Communist party, Zhdanov carried out a reform designed to guarantee individual rights of the Communists, reaffirming and strengthening rules to be observed in the case of expulsion, and so on.[87]

But there are no guarantees — traditional or legal — that these rules will always be regarded as binding on the rulers. Attempts to put the Secret Police under strict legal control have always failed. The Secret Police has always retained a form of purely administrative justice which assumes that the police bureaucracy is always right and the accused always wrong. Three-man boards, utilizing files in which denunciations and forced confessions have been collected,

57

condemn men to labor camps without giving the accused any chance to defend themselves. This is done even today although the death penalty has been abolished. Permissions from the prosecutor, which the law prescribes for the political police, are pure formalities; they are never refused. The ruling authorities ceaselessly issue general orders and regulations in an effort to counteract all arbitrary actions. A constant strife between such arbitrary actions and efforts at legal security characterizes the Soviet regime. This conflict cannot be resolved by an appeal to doctrine, however, since the doctrine itself sustains the unlimited power of the Soviet rulers. Lenin saw unhampered power as the essence of dictatorship, including the dictatorship of the proletariat.

As the second most important feature influencing the internal development of the Soviet state there must be mentioned the decreased expectation that outside revolutions would affect the Soviet regime. Weaker and weaker became the belief, prevalent during the first months after the October Revolution, that the rise of the Soviet regime was a signal for the immediate onset of the world revolution. Talk about the solidarity of the proletarians in all countries degenerated into a ritualistic formula. What happens outside the Soviet Union is evaluated exclusively on the basis of Soviet interests; the demands and expectations of world revolution are determined by the needs of Soviet foreign policy. The necessity of maintaining and expanding the power of the Soviet regime is expressed in Marxian terminology, for the realization of Socialism and Communism is made dependent upon the existence of the Soviet Union. Its enemies are necessarily enemies of socialism. All humanitarian considerations, all rights of individuals and communities, and all freedoms are subordinated to the power of the Soviet Union. There are no fundamental rights which limit this power. These are only means in the service of the security of the Soviet Union. All rights enumerated in the Stalin Constitution terminate when the existence of the Soviet regime or the rule of the Communist party is believed to be imperiled. There can be no strikes in the Soviet Union, for a strike would be directed against a regime which controls and directs economic life always in the true interest of the toiling masses. All papers, publications, associations must be under the control of the party and its government whose actions always serve the people. There can be no independent unions, for it must be the duty of the unions to serve the policies of the Soviet government, the government of the working population.[88] Religious groups are tolerated only because the social roots of religious beliefs are not yet extirpated; and even if their propaganda value is recognized and the election of the Patriarch of the Orthodox Church is again permitted, they are allowed to exist only under strict supervision by state organs.[89]

The promise of the doctrine that a perfect society will develop in which there will be only an administration of economic affairs in the interest of all and with participation of all, without violence and coercion, has not been fulfilled. This promised society of total liberty, satisfying everyone's needs, has not emerged. But the totalitarian state has come to pass, holding all power over all the realms of life in its hands. It is precisely the Marxian-Bolshevik belief in the withering away of the state as a class-instrument of coercion which justifies this expansion of power. The dictatorship of the proletariat is required in order to abolish the existence of all classes and therefore of the proletariat itself. The totalitarian state appears necessary to establish a total, self-regulating society without state and without coercion. But the coming of this society is postponed to an ever more distant future date. The present is dominated by the unlimited power of the totalitarian state — absolutely required, as Stalin has reiterated, in a period when enemies besiege the Soviet Union. The totalitarian state is also necessary to accomplish, in accelerated tempo, the industrialization that will overcome (according to the official doctrine) the backward agrarian character of the Union. It is not by chance that those Soviet jurists and students of political sociology like Pashukanis, who, with Lenin, emphasized that the withering away of the state would accompany the dictatorship of the proletariat, have been liquidated.[90]

The Totalitarian Party

The total state is an instrument of the party. Fundamental for

59

the Soviet regime is the identification of the party with the true will of the masses, a will formulated by the party, often in contradiction to moods and feelings deemed transitory or derived from wrong and hostile influences and the surviving elements of the past. The party is the "avant-garde" of the masses of the proletariat, and its general political line is always right, even though mistakes in details might occur. But this line is as infallible as the general will of Jean Jacques Rousseau.

The party directs and determines everything — the Soviets, the government and its machinery, the doctrine (both as to its formulation and interpretation), and finally the individual party members themselves. The battle cry of 1917, "All power to the Soviets," under which the Bolsheviks conquered Russia, resulted in the party's total conquest of power. Despite the fiction continued in the Stalin Constitution, it does not matter that the Soviets — today the so-called Supreme Soviet — have the ultimate decisive power.[91] This ultimate power rests really in the hands of the party. A Soviet congress has never acted against the will of the party; no one has ever been elected a member of the government by the Supreme Soviet without the previous approval of the party. Stalin determined Soviet policies before he became chairman of the Council of People's Commissars in 1941. From 1927, after the destruction of the opposition block of Trotsky-Zinoviev, he had a controlling position in the party. Members of the leading party organ, the Politburo, determined policies before they became cabinet members or deputies of Stalin, the chief of the government. Despite the reforms of Zhdanov after the great purge (1936-1938), the rights of the Communists in practice are limited to give to the party members only such legal guarantees as recognized by committees whose membership is renewed by self-perpetuation or appointments from above. The party leadership determines the composition of all party organs. It can exclude individuals from the party and accordingly organize the composition of the party congress which, as the supreme organ of the party, elects the central committee. The central committee, which selects the members of the highest policy-making organs — the politburo, the organizational board and the secretariat — approve the expulsion of its own members.[92]   Therefore Stalin's method of reaching power consisted first in controlling the delegates and then in gaining the support of the majority of the so-called plenum of the Central Committee when it was called together.   The party statute is not strictly observed.   Although there is a prescription for a party congress every two years, the last party congress met in 1939.

The conclusive power of the leaders is camouflaged by the slogan "democratic centralism," which would give the impression that obedience is due to elected leaders.   But the real power in the party is not determined by the vote of party delegates or by the party congress, but by the fact that between the party congresses the elected organs can change their own composition.   Therefore, whoever controls them controls all party elections.   In Lenin's time the domination of the leading organs over the party was not yet fully developed and streamlined, although under Lenin, in the party congress of 1921, the formation of factions among Communists was forbidden — a measure which became the basis for the fight against any criticism of the party leadership.   But owing to his extraordinary authority, acquired not only as the party founder but as the man who had successfully led the party into power, Lenin was always able to master oppositions, only rarely resorting to such means as arrest.   At the beginning of the regime there was obviously no machinery available to organize bloody purges.   This situation changed as Stalin acquired power, although the extension of the use of violence and pressure (applied to the world outside the party) to the party and its members did not become a practice until years after Stalin had taken over control of the Bolshevik party.

Stalin achieved his position as the master only after prolonged struggles and complicated maneuvers that played one group against the other.[93]   As long as Lenin was able to participate in political life (down to 1922) Stalin was only one under-leader among many, though he was used as a kind of trouble shooter.   Other collaborators of Lenin — particularly Trotsky — were much better known than Stalin; and regardless of a few cliques supporting Stalin, Trotsky had the control of the army.   Stalin's rise to power began in 1922 when upon the proposal of Zinoviev he was appointed secretary-general. The party secretariat had been regarded as a technical office; but Stalin knew how to utilize it for building up a machine to be at his own disposal. The attempts of the dying Lenin to limit Stalin's power came too late. Stalin cooperated first with Trotsky's competitors, Kamenev and Zinoviev; the composition of the party membership was changed by the acceptance of new members, the so-called *Leninskij prisyv*. Kamenev and Zinoviev discovered too late that they were no longer necessary to Stalin. Stalin could afford to deprive them of all power and finally to expel them from the party along with Trotsky, with whom they had now formed a bloc.

A few years later the rightist opposition, whose leaders, Bukharin, Rykov and Tomski, had supported the secretary-general in his campaign against Trotsky-Zinoviev, was destroyed. The leaders of all opposition groups accepted more or less humbly the party line and received posts of secondary importance. Trotsky was expelled from the Soviet Union.

Not until 1936 did Stalin, who had in accordance with Lenin's advice refused to cross the bloodline in the party (he had rejected Zinoviev's demand to liquidate Bukharin),[94] decide to apply bloody terror systematically against leading party members. Zinoviev and Kamenev, who had been arrested and sentenced to prison terms after the assassination of Stalin's lieutenant politburo-member, Kirov, were now executed after a trial: they confessed publicly in a most abject way their crimes against the party and the Soviet regime. That was the beginning of a purge of the party as well as of all branches of government; not only were the real enemies of Stalin made victims but also any and all officials who might be potential enemies or who had become unpopular for their role in the collectivization of agriculture, as members of the secret police, and so on. The great purge completed ruthlessly the development of the party under Stalin. Intellectuals, former émigrés, who had played an important role in the first years of the regime, were eliminated. They were replaced by men of practical interests, disinclined to hesitation, doubt, or theoretical discussion. The feeling of complacency and security inside the party was destroyed; absolute loyalty and obedience to the leaders at the top and particularly to the immovable leader became the main virtue, superseding and obscuring all claims based on merits of the past. Even before the purge, Stalin had dissolved the associations of old Bolsheviks which had given them privileged rights. After its bloody phase was over, the purge continued in the form of general insecurity inside the party, giving the younger generations chances to obtain leading positions.

The terror inside the party was an antidote to the consequences of its bureaucratization. The routine and clumsiness of the party bureaucracy had to be overcome by policies showing the limited function of all legal rules and traditions. The terror inside the party demonstrated the totalitarian essence of the Soviet regime, the unlimited, naked nature of its power justified by the official doctrine. The execution of such men as Yagoda, who had for sixteen years exercised leadership over the police, proved that no sub-lieutenant and assistant of Stalin was secure.

Lenin had educated the revolutionary intellectuals to be professional revolutionaries. Stalin now replaced professional revolutionaries by "apparatschiks," brutal robots in the service of the power and policies of the party as formulated and ordered by its infallible, deified leadership. The basic feature of the Bolshevik terror reappear also inside the party. This terror is an impersonal one. Personal hate and revenge play in practice a great role; Stalin himself liked to humiliate and liquidate his personal enemies and those whose background as intellectuals (who despised him) he resented. But most important is its technical orientation: man is not seen as a person but as material for the maintenance and for the increase of might and domination. The party itself becomes an instrument of this development — only the leader remains a kind of ultimate point of orientation, representing the true doctrine and the true tradition. Lenin, the disciple of Marx and the inventor of the tactics appropriate for an imperialist epoch, is the master of Stalin, who has become, as leader of the U.S.S.R. and its party, the great teacher and leader of "progressive" mankind in our time.

The Control by the Minority and Its Methods

The Soviet regime is a system in which a well-organized minority controls all power. The leaders of the dominating party take care that persons and groups designated as useless or known as actively or potentially hostile to their exclusive controls, are liquidated. If such liquidation proves inexpedient, as in the instance of the Orthodox Church, these elements are deprived of independence and are closely supervised.

The omnipresent and all-embracing terror and pressure are directed not only against real enemies of the regime, that is, such persons as have committed hostile acts against the Soviet government, but against anyone declared to be an enemy. Those arrested by the Security Police — called today MVD — must regard themselves as guilty; for the representatives of the regime cannot be wrong. The function of terror and pressure is to show the limitless, unrestrained power of the regime — which does not stop, as the purges prove, even at the level of the party and the members of its highest organs — for also members of the Politburo, like Kossior and Rudzutak, have been liquidated. Rudzutak was not helped by his being appointed in 1933 to the chairmanship of a special commission for a party purge. Anybody can be a spy in the service of the police on the one hand, and on the other hand, anybody can be dealt with as if he were an enemy of the regime. This creates uncertainty and distrust as well as the feeling of being completely dependent on the masters of the regime; and only one of these masters seems to be himself above suspicion and uncertainty — Stalin, the wise leader of the Soviet Union and guide of all peoples. The ubiquitous terror ensures the acceptance of the Soviet world as a reality which cannot be opposed and whose policies must be publicly accepted in spite of all the violations of rules and all the corruptions which constantly occur and without which life would be unbearable or even impossible.

The spread of these violations and corruptions can be checked only by sudden terrorist interventions. But the terrorist methods, the liquidations of high officials (MVD victims often meet later their pitiless judges and prosecutors in the labor camps) do not reduce illegal actions and corruption in its various forms.[95] Any attempt to oppose the system as such appears hopeless and meaningless, for it seems that there can be no other reality than that of the almighty Soviet regime which has no respect for anyone's dignity or past merits.

A second decisive means by which the Soviet system becomes a reality from which there can be no escape, is the monopoly of propaganda. This propaganda would exploit for its purpose the regime's display of the power and the exclusive "truth" of its doctrine in all realms of life.[96] Even apparently quite apolitical activities are evaluated and utilized according to their function in and importance for the power and policies of the regime. No realm is safe from party orders and interventions: Church life, sports, cultural and scientific work, all means of communication (press, radio, movies), must serve the propaganda. Its slogans, bound to determine all activities and interests, are spread not only by staffs of party organizers and agitators, but by all groups, institutions and activities. There can be no neutrality or indifference towards it. Those who do not spread the propaganda — for example, scientific publications, academic institutions, and writers rejecting a utilitarian concept of art — are regarded as enemies of the regime.

A passive acceptance or silent toleration of orders and the official general line of the party is not sufficient. The Soviet regime is not authoritarian, but totalitarian; it endeavors to appear as the mouthpiece of the masses which it activates with the help of the propaganda slogans, which are at the same time beacons for action in the right direction. For the monopoly and all-permeating character of the official propaganda are justified by the doctrinal claim that the party alone has the true theory and that its leadership is the authoritative organ of its interpretations not only through pronouncements, but also through actions and policies. For theory and action form a unity, it is emphasized again and again, following Marx's famous formula that his aim is not to interpret the world but to change it.

Obviously, this all-embracing totalitarian propaganda with its

65

intended monopoly could not have been realized from the beginning of the regime. But even before he took power Lenin regarded it as a self-evident necessity. He had always fought his adversaries as personifying basic errors and deviations; for him they were not only political opponents but vicious heretics.[97] After the seizure of power by his party it became possible to suppress the propaganda and the organizations of its adversaries and of non-Bolsheviks; the hostile press was forbidden, and uncontrolled public demonstrations of any kind were outlawed. Despite the building up of Bolshevik propaganda, however, neutral institutions and cultural-artistic activities had to be tolerated for years. Under a Bolshevik like Riazanov who retained a belief in the solidarity of scientific research workers and had some soft-hearted understanding of non-Bolshevik socialists, some Menshevik experts worked even in his Marx-Engels Institute, which lost its significance after his removal and exile. Even the Academy of Science remained for a long time untouched. But all this was only the lull before the storm. From the thirties on, the party began to realize its totalitarian claims over cultural activities. The works of the historian Pokrovsky, who had been hitherto regarded as Marxian and authoritative, were condemned by the Central Committee, which issued basic prescriptions for historical writing. Similar battles were fought against deviations on the philosophical front.[98] Through the reorganization of their groups, writers were required to submit to the politics and economics of the regime. Even the doctrines of the natural sciences were prescribed in the name of the party line. This assumption by the party of complete control of intellectual and cultural life and of all scientific institutions was related to the fact that, after the regime of Lunatscharsky as commissar of education of the Russian Soviet Republic was ended, the party became more and more hostile to all modernistic and experimental attitudes which formerly had been favored. Factual knowledge and strict discipline, combined with the recognition of the unlimited competence of the classics of Marxism — Marx and Engels as authoritatively interpreted by the two other classics Lenin and Stalin — were now stressed in the official line. Totalitarian control was completed after World War II, as Zhdanov, on behalf of the party leadership, imposed pre-scribed attitudes and views upon writers, musicians, and scientists.[99] Stalin's celebrated ultimate authority in all fields was shown by his letters of 1950 on linguistic problems, which reorganized the "philo-logical front" and destroyed the domination of that field held by the late Soviet academician Marr.[100] All research, all writing, all education must be in the service of the governing party, a policy per-mitting the party to control not only the state but all public and intellectual life.

This policy is likewise expressed by the party attitude towards religion. The party knows that frontal attacks against what it re-gards as anti-scientific superstition, as well as the imprisonment and execution of Church leaders as counter-revolutionaries, are unsuc-cessful measures. Accordingly, the official Soviet policy has re-versed itself so as to deal with the Churches as Institutions con-trolled by the state. The Orthodox Church serves as its political in-strument; its head, the Patriarch of Moscow, is used to weaken Ukrainian nationalism by putting an end to an independent auton-omous Ukrainian Church and to weaken the influence of the Papacy. The Ukrainian Greek Catholic Church, recognizing the authority of the Roman pontiff, has been forced to accept the authority of the head of the Russian Orthodox Church.

It would be erroneous to think that the omnipresent terror and the monopoly of totalitarian propaganda result in inflexible policies. Up to now the leadership of the Bolshevik party has masterfully handled without losing initiative and control the art of taking into account the moods and instincts of the masses. The party doctrine refuses, on the one hand, to act as a "tail" of the masses (the heresy of so-called Khvostism); on the other hand, it asserts that the actions of the party must correspond to the true will of the masses. Thus, "putschism" and "blanquism," which believe that a small minority without mass support is capable of carrying out a successful revolution, are bluntly condemned. Accommodations to the mood of the masses is evident in a number of measures: the introduction of the NEP, a retreat from war communism (which Lenin, impressed by the sailor revolt in Kronstadt and local peasant

67

uprisings, deemed necessary); Stalin's famous appeal to stop the overzealous forced collectivization of agriculture in 1931; the general turn towards Soviet nationalism leading to a Great Russian nationalism after the war, as mirrored in Stalin's famous praise of the Russians as the hegemonial people; and the fight against cosmopolitans and local chauvinists oblivious of the merits and the historical role of the Russian proletariat or devoted abjectly to the foreign world of the West.

All these adaptations, however, are determined by power political considerations and tactics. They do not go beyond certain limits; they do not touch the utter monopoly of control by the party — that is, of the party leadership. No one should be deceived by adaptations and changes in institutions and policies, like the abandonment of easy divorces and the emphasis upon a stable family,[101] or the open return to a strong authoritarian state with a hierarchical order according to services, symbolized in the restoration of traditional titles (minister, general, and so on). The absolute party monopoly is still maintained, with the help of the official Marxian-Leninist-Stalinist political religion. The secular political religion justifies any and all alterations and maneuvers; it expresses a belief in the continuity and the necessary mission of the regime; it makes every inhuman action seem an unavoidable means of realization of the coming perfect society, and the sacrifices and sufferings of the present as imperfections of a transitional period. The secular religion systematically explains away the contradictions between doctrine and practice as the consequences both of the inherited backwardness of the Soviet Union (to be overcome at all costs) and of the constant pressure exercised by capitalist-imperialist enemies outside and inside its frontiers.

The Character of the Party Elite

But what is this totalitarian elite, the Bolshevik party, in reality? Its particular character can be grasped only if we distinguish it from the elites of the Tsarist regime on the one side, and the utopian revolutionaries on the other side.

Different from the Tsarist ruling elites, the party of Lenin-

Stalin does not know any traditional limitations upon its actions. Its conscious belief that it is the instrument of a necessary development of society produces a basic attitude: everything that promotes the conquest, maintenance and expansion of its own power is permissible. The revolutionary rejection of traditionalism in the name of Marxism plays the same role today as did its rejection in the eighteenth century by Peter the Great, who as a brutal autocrat felt strong enough to hazard the construction of a new order. The combination of anti-traditionalism and of a missionary zeal, based upon "objectively" necessary developments, illuminates the methods by which relations are regulated not only with the outside world but with party members themselves. The party — and that means the victorious party leadership able to impose its policies — is always right; under-leaders and agents can always be sacrificed, accused and liquidated as traitors, when this action serves the purposes of power. The party leadership determines what the facts are, what composes true tradition, history, science and freedom; it rejects and discredits former defeated party leaders, from Trotsky to Radek, as imperialist spies; it practically obliterates their names. If such names are mentioned occasionally, they are represented as symbols of dark and evil forces — that is the treatment given Trotsky in the official textbook on the *History of the Communist Party of the Soviet Union*.[102] Remarkable indeed are the schematic formulas of speech and thought which, going back to usages developed by the Russian revolutionary intelligentsia, have been perfected in Bolshevik literature and propaganda. In order to present Russian experiences as universally significant, such words as "Trotskyism," "liquidators"— most recently "Titoism"— are applied to situations everywhere from the United States to China.[103] Attempts are repeatedly made to prove that all countries will have to imitate Soviet policies, for example, in their relation to the peasants. Of course, the party leadership decides which situations are analogous and which Soviet policies must be applied at the moment. Therefore, parallels with events and methods in the history of the Soviet party are purely terminological in character; their meaning and their selection are dictated by Moscow. The apparently "objective" historical approach serves to increase the power and influence of the party leadership at home and of the Soviet leadership in the communist movement throughout the world. This unlimited power of the Bolshevik leadership over the true interpretation of docrtine and action prevents the rise of a closed ruling group. The better chances for education and careers possessed by children of party officials and bureaucrats are balanced by the prevailing insecurity. Those who are at the top today are in disgrace tomorrow, victims of a change in the party line or of a "self-criticism," often scapegoats for political and economic failures. Obviously, cynicism and ruthlessness together with subservience to those at the top are favored by such an atmosphere; the formation of an hereditary elite is impossible, though exceptions to this rule, like the military career of the son of Stalin, may be cited.

The Bolshevik party is distinguished from a merely utopian revolutionary movement by its ability to take into consideration the existing relations of power and to apply and elaborate techniques and methods of focusing, developing and utilizing its own iron power, while weakening, dissipating and confusing the power of the opposite camp. Lenin always emphasizes how needful it is to learn from capitalism and its experience. He once remarked that "capitalism must be used in order to build socialism." But it is obvious that bourgeois non-Communist specialists are used only so long as the Communists themselves do not have the required skills, so long as the young Communist generation has not yet grown up.

The regime is constantly threatened by the danger of purely mechanical education. Obedience to the leaders and blind acceptance of the general line are esteemed infinitely more than initiative and independent personal judgment. For all social and political questions are regarded only as power problems to be solved by technical skill as soon as the necessary cadres are available. General questions are thought to receive their answers in the formulas of political religion. The history of the development from Lenin to Stalin shows how the technician-manipulator, a skilled expert in a special field—substituting fixed schemes and ritualistic slogans for universal knowledge and culture—replaces those revolutionaries to whom socialism meant more than the concentration of might and ruthless organization. Socialism was in their eyes related to freedom and justice, even in the present transitional period. Such an attitude has become outdated; its representatives, if they have survived, have lost any influence. Bolshevism regards lack of discipline, that is, of subservience to the authoritative interpreters of the doctrine, as anarchism which has to be destroyed.

Bolshevism in the Russian Environment

What has the Soviet regime accomplished during the thirty-four years of its existence?

Many important achievements of modern civilization have been brought to Russia. At the expense of tradition and custom as well as of the needs of consumers, technical methods have been introduced and industrialization speeded up. This turn to the material aspects of the western world was effected in drastic fashion. The collectivization of agriculture, increasing the use of machinery, erecting motor tractor stations, and so on, was accomplished at the cost of millions of exiles and deaths. Many unexploited regions in the North have been opened up with the help of those condemned to forced labor and compelled to perform their tasks under conditions so deleterious to health that an extraordinarily high death rate resulted.[104] The interest in the individual and in his welfare, the consideration for workers and consumers, which have accompanied, whatever the brutalities, periods of capitalist rise (the Marxian primary "accumulation") and of colonial exploitation, are here subordinated to the need for results. The party executive who masters modern administrative and technical methods, who is not deflected by sentimental humanitarian considerations from fulfilling and over-fulfilling the plan, stands as the ideal type of the regime. That everything is oriented to the operation of industrial plants and to a maximum increase of production is illustrated by the role assigned to the labor unions in the Soviet Union. They are not supposed to represent and protect the interests of the worker (for example, to call strikes); they exist to help the management in the fulfillment

71

of its plans. And there can be no strikes, for economic life is dominated by a party and government which claim to act always in the interest of the masses.

One of the historical factors bringing about the power of Bolshevism in Russia was the antagonism between the western elites and the masses little touched by Western reforms and mentality. The disappearance of the traditional authority, the tsar-emperor, permitted the collapse and dissolution of the political-social order. The westernized intellectuals and politicians of liberal and moderate-socialist parties had no authority; their power was only a pseudo-power. The sailors killed their officers;[105] the soldiers deserted; the workers rebelled against any discipline; the peasants waited for the hour to take over the land of the estate owners. On the other hand, the representatives of the "party of order," who tried to impose the strong man General Kornilov on the country, were too much discredited by the remembrance of things past. The masses wanted revenge for the sufferings and restraints imposed upon them. And the forced abdication of Nicholas II had dissolved the forces and habits which kept the masses subservient.

Power to impose order and obedience was to be snatched on the streets. Lenin was able to acquire this power because in 1917 he knew how to exploit in his movement's favor the constantly spreading anarchy, and then to replace — as he announced — the bearers of the old authority, the 100,000 estate owners, with members of the Bolshevik party.[106] In the interest of the masses Bolsheviks declared their dedication to a necessary social development and to its acceleration by every possible means. After the brief period of explosive anarchy, permitting the wildest fluidity in all political and social relations, there followed the building up of totalitarian control of the whole of life. The utopian elements, very important in the period of anarchy and very suitable for the destruction of traditional institutions and groups, began to recede more and more in the face of the necessities of power politics employing the appropriate political and technical means. Totalitarian control, beginning with the October Revolution, was perfected and completed under Stalin. The introduction of five-year plans, the destruction of the independent peasantry, and the systematic exploitation of forced labor marked this development.

The Bolsheviks knew how to discredit their adversaries, either as warmongers or as advocates of a return of the state owners, and how to play one group against the other. The systematic character of their policy was not understood; momentary tactical concessions were believed to be definitive and permanent ones. The Bolsheviks were able to organize, develop and entrench their party as an instrument of domination without abandoning the original doctrine and terminology.[107] The party eliminated on the one side elements unfit for practical rule, like intellectuals preoccupied with theories and discussions; and on the other side it placed non-Bolshevik "specialists" in the service of the regime. The party has succeeded in creating around itself a vacuum which apparently does not admit anything other than the Bolshevik rule. The unknown opposition, unable to manifest itself in public or to assume an organized form, is composed of individuals and groups who must, on the surface at least, enthusiastically accept and support the Soviet government. Only a limited criticism of the execution of the general line is permitted for the sake of increasing the insecurity[108] of sub-leaders and of giving the appearance of spontaneity; but the elimination of all resistance and basic criticism does not satisfy the totalitarian Stalinist rule. Not even a constant display of fanatical approval and participation, always "spontaneous" and "voluntary," suffices for the regime. The all-embracing power of the system must be demonstrated by constant purges, new plans, feverish drives and incessant reorganizations.

By the monopoly of propaganda permeating every realm of life, and by the eternal threat of a relentless terrorism, an atmosphere is generated throughout society which makes the individual an isolated being confronted by the gigantic power machinery and completely at the mercy of the masters. The engineers of this machinery never let it stop. The masses as well as the individuals composing them steadily receive new duties and directions. Their forces and energies are always kept in motion; no time for reflection and contemplation is permitted; everything must be directed and dominated by the orders of the totalitarian masters. The very fact that the Soviet regime is in many respects backward, that modern techniques must be learned and industrialization pushed forward so as to approach the levels of other countries, is utilized to keep alive and to stimulate drives and pressures. The capitalist environment is made responsible for every imperfection, and for the reactionary traitors and weaklings influenced by it. Encircled by imperialist powers, the Soviet Union must always remain mistrustful so as always to be able to resist conspiracies and attacks.[109] It must always be strong enough to defeat interventions. There is an incessant appeal to pride over past and future accomplishments. Because the Soviet regime exists, it is now possible to overcome backwardness and to catch up with the most advanced countries of the world. Such arguments and slogans are used to stir to a maximum the energies of the masses. Expansions are always pictured as measures of defence against threatening aggression or as proofs of the internal weakening and decay of capitalist opponents.

The totalitarian Soviet regime is, in its leadership, free from paternalist and traditionalist elements; but its constant urge to activity and expansion is the product of a peculiar social situation, the result of historical developments. Groups without experience of modern industrialization are driven forward by a small "avant-garde" and provided with opportunities for advancement and social rise. This elite believes fanatically in the importance of technical achievement, in the deification of science, and in a "necessary" social development; but in a manner different from the paternalist-traditionalist Tsarist regime it exploits unlimitedly its absolute power.[110] Everything, including the fate and employment of the masses, the human material, becomes a purely technical power problem.

The service state of the Muscovite medieval period, in which status was assigned to everyone according to his function in the ruler's organization of defense, now reappears[111]— but in an infinitely and terrifyingly perfected form — owing to the use of modern technical and administrative methods. There are no gaps, no openings for escape. The socialization of the means of production is not only an economic step; it is a means of transforming all human existence, of putting man and society into the possession of the directors of socialization. Political religion shrinks into a formal justification of the necessary techniques of domination and of the artificial reality required for their unhampered application. The Tsarist mixture of an absolute rule with traditional and legal elements is replaced by a new totalitarian rule intensified by its peculiar combination of utopian elements and by its knowledge of how to manipulate the masses. Power engineering replaces the traditionalist features of the ancient regime.

It would be quite erroneous to accept Bolshevik self-interpretation and to believe that the Soviet regime came into existence as the culmination of a necessary process of development. Actually it rose from an unpredictable combination of the crisis of the Tsarist regime in the midst of a world war and its skillful exploitation by Lenin.[112] Without Lenin the Bolsheviks would not have come into power; and it is important to remember that Lenin's most difficult task in 1917 was to impose his policies upon his party. A unique situation existed; unexpected objective conditions and social tendencies were exploited by a leader presenting his fight for power as the realization of a "necessary" development of history. And Lenin succeeded not only in reaching power but in keeping it. The fluid situation aiding his rise changed into a period of stabilization. The era of anarchy, called by the Bolsheviks that of "revolutionary enthusiasm," was replaced by the period of the foundation and stabilization of a new order. This system of rule, backed by terror and totalitarian control and allowing all kinds of policy-shifts, vanquished every attempt to oppose or destroy it. It mattered little whether these attempts were undertaken by disappointed Communists like Trotsky or by individualist revolutionaries fighting Lenin's and Stalin's bureaucratic machine[113] or by peasants refusing to be simple tools after the enforced collectivization of agriculture. Totalitarian absolutism in the name of political secular religion proved to be infinitely more efficient than the authoritarian absolutism of the Tsars, checked as they were by paternalist considerations and at least by some traditional respect for human life.

75

Attempts made in the period between the downfall of Tsarism and the rise of Bolshevism to introduce into Russia western liberal-democratic institutions and techniques of rule did not succeed because of the contradiction between the demand for using peaceful-legal methods and the revolutionary origin of the Provisional Government. The revolution went the whole way from anarchical dissolution to the setting-up of a completely totalitarian regime without a vestige of respect for legal methods and humanitarian-liberal traditions. The drive for power by Lenin and the party following his line defeated a policy of reforms which seemed able neither to satisfy the elemental wishes of the masses nor to stop the spread of anarchy. Lenin and the Bolsheviks took over. And the historic hour of pure power politics, mobilizing and utilizing the masses, began.

War as the Normal Situation

For the Soviet regime (looking upon itself as an instrument of a necessary and ethical development opposed by a hostile world), unceasing tensions and a status of perpetual war must appear as normal. Dialectical development means uninterrupted changes. Crises, produced by the successes of the regime as well as by the aggressive distrust of internal and external enemies, nourish an attitude of vigilance and fear. Campaigns follow one after the other; at best they are interrupted by brief pauses and armistices in order to gather new strength for the advance which has to come. The New Economic Policy (NEP) had as its aim no change in the basic policies of the regime but rather the organization and assemblage of forces in a renewed effort to realize socialism and totalitarian planning. Stalin acted as the loyal successor of Lenin when he ended the pause of the NEP with a new attack: the compulsory collectivization of agriculture, in opposition to the "rightists," Rykov-Bukharin and Tomski, who wanted to satisfy the peasants and rejected a policy of coercion against them.[114] Party purges followed. Stalin's bloody purge was the culmination of a system introduced by Lenin, though it is true that only expulsions, but not executions, of party members occurred under Lenin. Victory in the second World War did not bring a continuation of the war years' policies, which kept the party in the background and emphasized the patriotic character of the struggle against the rapacious Nazi aggressors.[115]   After 1945 the leaders of the Soviet regime insist again upon the importance of the party, the necessity of indoctrination, of strengthening totalitarian controls, and of distrusting the capitalist-imperialist powers.   Wartime cooperation — accepted for military reasons — is replaced by the cold war against the United States and the West.   And it is typical that Zhdanov carried out policies enforcing the party's control over all intellectual and cultural activities — even those which seem completely apolitical, like botany and music.

In the period after 1945, the totalitarian regime intensifies itself by appeals and the selection of symbols which change according to need.   Scorn and hate are directed against everything non-Soviet and non-Russian.   This naive and primitive glorification of the Soviet Union and its background, the history of the Empire erected by the Tsars,[116] corresponds to the instincts of the masses and flatters them.

This Soviet nationalism is a particularly striking illustration of the general development undergone by the Soviet regime.   More and more emphasis is put on means.   In the name of the coming humanity in which every need of every individual will be taken care of and in which the state, today the instrument of coercion, will wither away, groups and individuals are dealt with today as material evaluated and employed according to simple technical considerations.   Sacrifices of the consumers in our time are excused or required by the prospect of a good and easy life once the socialist construction is accomplished and the capitalist environment has evaporated.

The fact that the Marxian doctrine does not offer details about the coming society, and that the party must constantly learn from experiences in the more and more extended period of transformation, permits a variety of methods.   It would be wrong to ascribe this attitude exclusively to Stalin.   Lenin, for example, was ready

77

to accept the agrarian program of the Socialist Revolutionaries (SR) when power-calculations made it advisable in 1917. Though he trifled with utopian economic schemes, he declared the need for experience and discipline, for studious attention to capitalist achievements. It may be, however, that in its duration the regime has become somewhat ossified. Past experiences, like the NEP, collectivization, the handling of opposition-groups, have become general standards which are simply accepted and applied again and again; whereas, for Lenin and Stalin (in the first periods of his power) these were bold and risky actions rather than straight-jacket formulas.

Lack of hesitation in choice of means and methods marked Lenin from his younger days. In his effort to destroy the enemy which was most dangerous at the moment he did not fear to avail himself of the strangest associates. During the *Iskra* period (1900-1903) he took advantage of liberal-bourgeois criticism of those who wanted to direct the labor movement towards social reforms minus political-revolutionary aims. The Bolshevik party always regarded itself as an army which understood its goal and could involve in its battles the oddest auxiliaries — auxiliaries which could be dropped, destroyed, and replaced when no longer needed. The allies of today were the enemies of tomorrow, and the enemies of today the allies of tomorrow. Various approaches, that is, policies, could be used to storm the fortresses first of Tsarism and then of Capitalism. What has increased in the years of the Soviet regime is not cynicism and amoralism but the acceptance of set formulas and schemes: Soviet experiences have become ritualized and canonized; new approaches and maneuvers are deemed out of question; the circle of experience is closed; experiments which would bring unexpected results are believed impossible.

Some critiques of the Bolshevik-Stalinist regime have tried to combine a rejection of its terrorist-inhuman methods with an acceptance of its historical role and accomplishments.[117] Stalin's policies, it is asserted, have resulted in a modernization and industrialization of backward Russia, illiteracy has almost disappeared, production increased, and so on. This apologia overlooks the fact that modernization and industrialization were developing before 1917. N. S. Timasheff, particularly, has shown us this, citing an ample collection of facts. Hence the question is: what human and material sacrifices have the compulsory acceleration and total planning under the Soviet regime demanded? This question reminds us of the attitude of Karl Marx in *Das Kapital,* where he presents a dark picture of a rising capitalism employing inhuman methods of expropriation and of destruction of the pre-capitalist classes. Careful observers like Harry Schwartz have stated that Soviet industrialization has been paid for with enormous suffering and sacrifices. These, he notes, would not have been nearly so high had the erection of new plants, the exploitation of hitherto unexplored territories, the introduction of modern machinery and the reorganization of trade not been enforced from above by methods which subordinated the needs of consumers to the building up of industrial might for the sake of Russian independence and military strength.[118] The millions of victims of the collectivization of agriculture and of the labor camps can be cited as impressive proofs of the human cost of the regime, even if one does not accept fully Jasny's elaborate demonstrations of lowering of living standards as a result of the collectivization of agriculture.

But have not young, efficient leaders replaced the old decadent, inefficient Tsarist bureaucracy and elites? Lenin's sharp criticism of Soviet bureaucracy in 1922 could be repeated today. Fear of responsibility and initiative, meaningless, inhuman, mechanical application of rules, over-emphasis upon loyalty and obedience to the Stalinist leadership — not to speak of the corruption alone making life possible — characterize Soviet bureaucracy in the party as well as in the government. The situation is more uncertain than it was under the Tsarist regime since there are no lasting legal guarantees, and since application of the law can always be over-ruled by a totalitarian political power much more efficient and drastic than that of the authoritarian Tsarist regime. True, a certain pressure is created by means of "self-criticism" directed not against the general line and the party leadership but against the executors of policies.[119] But this self-criticism can become itself a

79

terrorist means of spreading insecurity. Nobody knows when or under what circumstances he will become the object of this self-criticism. To avoid the worst, everybody becomes willing to make abject confessions and to promise improvement in behavior.

The duration of the Soviet regime is made possible by the un-limited power of its leaders, a power exercised according to careful technical considerations of efficiency. If Stalin and his colleagues in the Politburo were merely erratic tyrants interested exclusively in displaying their power and satisfying their whims without any thought of the existing circumstances, their rule would have collapsed a long time ago. They must constantly fight against a bureaucratization which threatens the regime by a senseless appli-cation of rules, by bogging down in the morass of routine, and by a mixture of inefficiency and corruption. Totalitarian power and terror compensate for the lack of public spirit. At first it was enough to apply them to the world outside the party; it became necessary, however, as the regime endured and the number of enthusiastic supporters believing in a utopia decreased, to use them inside the party also. A second means of keeping things going consists of psychological appeals and stimulants. This explains the hierarchical character of Soviet society: the hierarchical order enables the Soviet citizen to know the exact compensation by uni-forms, medals, variation in facilities, even by grants of food for various degrees of "merit."[120] On the other hand, the Soviet hierarchy is not dominated by a closed hereditary elite; up to now its rise has been prevented by the general insecurity and social in-stability. Anybody can be demoted at any time, and the plight of his family follows his fate. Paternalist, traditionalist attitudes are frustrated by this kind of instability. Consequently, there is an unceasing, crushing fight for position and power. The official doc-trine is the abstract point of orientation and Stalin is the personal embodiment of this point. The doctrine and Stalin cannot be separated: Stalin says what the doctrine is, and the doctrine says what Stalin is. Stalin and the doctrine are flexible enough to permit adaptations to new situations. Yet the system seems able to answer all questions, exclude all doubts and maintain a specific politico-social regime — a totalitarian regime without independent groups but with a maximum concentration of power, unity of political and economic control, appeals to the masses, hostility towards inherited power positions (like the white race in Asia), and a skillful manipulation of mass emotions ranging from dislike of war to a primitive supernationalism.

The Soviet regime is the regime of totalitarian power politics adapted to conditions deriving from Russian history. But the Soviet masters pretend that they want to realize the will of the masses everywhere. Their simplifications, their claims to have the key to all situations of history and society in the past, present, and future, appeal also to the non-Russian world tired of over-compli- cated problems and longing for clear-cut decisions. This world is impressed by the fact that Soviet claims are backed by fierce power and an apparent doctrinal consistency which is flexible but un- tainted by skepticism and relativist doubts. Despairing over its own vacillations, the non-Russian world is stunned by the boldness of the Soviet faith. It recognizes that Leninism-Stalinism is based upon root-principles of the modern secularized era like scientism, belief in evolution, inevitable perfection, and the limitless successes of technical social engineering. The devotion of the Soviet regime to the needs of Russian reality has not decreased its global appeal.

CHAPTER III

BOLSHEVISM AS WORLD POWER

The discrepancy between the promises of Bolshevism and the Soviet reality is not to be explained by some casual misfortune like the success of Stalin; Stalin, it is said, a bad-willed man of devious cunning, became heir to the allegedly humanitarian Lenin; his rise to power also was facilitated by the clumsiness of his adversaries who, like Trotsky, were unable to build a political machine and who underrated, to their own ruin, the inconspicuous secretary-general.

The contradiction between the theory and the reality of Bolshevism — a contradiction between a propagandized declared freedom and its present practical destruction — originates in the very essence of Bolshevism as a political secular pseudo-religion, and its wrong ideas of man and society. External changes, socialization of means of production, and constant pressures are believed to be capable of changing the nature of men, of turning man into a being who will be able without guidance, owing to his perfect social education and experience, to perform all functions in the community. With this perfection achieved, no authority will be necessary, for all decisions will deal with purely technical-administrative problems within everyone's competence. Rule by those who, as Communists, know the line of development, will wipe out all evil influences of the past and its representatives, and will teach the masses not only to be perfect citizens but to be expert in all fields. Specialist-groups, a bureaucracy as well as an army separated from the people, will disappear along with the state. The unrestricted use of force will be necessary during the period of transition — terror is employed by the dictatorship of the proletariat in order to abolish the necessity of coercion.[121]

But this transitional period becomes a permanent one; the promises of the future serve only to justify the present system of all-engulfing domination. The ruling elite gathers more and more power into its hands and constantly perfects the methods by which a minority (having exclusive control over all instruments of domination and influence) can maintain, without ever forgetting its political aims, its mastery over the life and work of the masses. The development and practice of the regime established by Lenin and continued by Stalin show this contradiction between the communist promise to abolish the power politics of a minority — which claims to express the will of the masses — and the Soviet reality, truly a system of total domination permitting no escape for the individual, making him a cog in the politico-social machine and even forcing him to praise his enslavement as a realization of freedom.[122] But this blatant and spectacular contradiction has not prevented Bolshevism from becoming a world power. Its rise to world power is owing not merely to its successes within Russia. It is impossible to explain its influence in the world as the result of terror and pressure alone, for outside the Soviet Union and its satellites there is no direct physical or psychological compulsion to accept the root-ideas of the Communist party and to promote its policies.

The Soviet Mythology

Bolshevism has become a world power not only because of its absolute domination in Russia or because of the Soviet victory in the second World War brought control over new and vast territories, but also because, in many respects, it meets widespread popular demands of the society of the twentieth century. For this reason it has helped to shape the fundamental political style after World War I.

Bolshevism has gained a world-reputation by its claiming to embody socialism and by branding the various moderate socialist groups and leaders as traitors and opportunists who sell out the socialist "total change" of society to the bourgeois imperialists and replace it by pseudo-reforms. In its official self-interpretation Bolshevism pretends to have realized socialism in the Soviet Union by abolishing the private ownership of the means of production and thereby abolishing classes. So Bolshevik policies appear to be the

84

fulfillment of the hopes of the socialist movement and parties across the world. This explains why in the first years after World War I old socialist parties like those in Germany and in France split; large groups were willing to accept membership in the Third International.[123] Intellectuals regarded the Soviet rule as a promising social experiment, even if they were critical of many of its methods. But they were ready to explain these errors away by ascribing them to the backwardness of Russia. The socialist parties of all nations were compelled to deal constantly with Soviet politics, for they claim to embody in the immediate present what the moderate socialists say will be the result of a long, slow development. The defeat of the various White armies, despite outside support and intervention,[124] increased the prestige of the Soviet leadership. It was helpful, too, for the Soviet regime to be opposed by men and circles customarily regarded by socialists and progressives as their enemies, as evil reactionaries, and as greedy imperialists.

Whatever the world's disappointments in the history of the Third International and the various Communist parties as a sequence of defeats, defections and splits, a Soviet mythology has arisen which identifies the Soviet Union with political and social progress and presents its foreign policies as an incessant fight against aggression and for peace. Bolshevism, as a political religion, attracts many who have lost their inherited faith but who cannot be satisfied with skepticism and relativism. Many others are favorably impressed by Soviet policies because they seem to be practical, bent on constructive activity, and eager to build up a new world.[125]

Soviet policies, further, rest upon a belief of reaching, through modern scientific education and organization, a perfect, man-controlled society. Many radical cultural and artistic experiments were made in the first decade of the Soviet regime; later under Stalin there was a turn to an uninspiring, utilitarian, pseudo-realism in art and to an old-fashioned concern with the teaching and learning of facts. The early experimentalism had impressed many writers and artists.[126] In general the Soviet Union appears to its admirers full of vitality, oriented towards the future, and capable of drawing the inert masses, fettered by their old masters and by their obsolete traditions, into the world of modern civilization. Before 1917 it was obviously impossible to represent the existing Russian regime as an exemplar or as a center of experiments leading to the coming progressive society. On the contrary, Tsarism appeared as the bulwark of negative and evil reaction. After the October Revolution an adulatory interest in Soviet rule could and did develop. The Soviet regime, with all its shortcomings, stood as the heir of socialist movements, trying seriously to fulfill their aspirations. This Soviet mythology, presenting programs and promises as accomplished facts, was born and grew to exercise great influence regardless of the many disappointments provoked by Soviet policies. It does not matter that many ex-Communists and friends of the Soviet Union are converted into energetic antagonists of their former faith of the "God that failed." [127] Though the Soviet Union has abolished many reforms praised as a proof of its progressive character,[128] the Soviet mythology continues to thrive. The disappointed victims of the past are constantly replaced by new victims. They admit — if they admit anything — that backward Russia must catch up in great haste and that the Soviet regime, surrounded by a world of merciless enemies, must neglect for the time being its progressive reforms.

Since the beginning of the Soviet regime, the same central objections have been made against it, but they have not destroyed its mythical fascination. It has been repeatedly said that the Soviet Union is the dictatorship of a small minority skilled in manipulating the masses, that it has imposed upon the workers the strictest discipline demanded by the process of industrialization, that it has required extraordinary sacrifices from consumers, that it has inaugurated agrarian policies making victims of millions, that all its apparent relaxations of power have been made solely for the continuation of a policy aiming at progressively tighter and more perfect totalitarian controls. The revelations about Soviet reality made by former Communists, and in many European countries by ex-prisoners of the Soviet armies, have diminished the prestige of Soviet Communism,[129] but the foundations of this prestige have not been shaken. Numerous intellectuals still look upon Soviet policies as policies of peace. Peoples and nations, dissatisfied with existing conditions (living standards, colonial policies, and the like) are still inclined to regard the Soviet Union as their ally and helper. The conviction that the Soviet Union, with all its errors, realizes social justice and socialism, remains alive. The naive, humanitarian progressive devotees of the Soviet regime are joined today by some cynics impressed by successful power politics and ready to praise Lenin and Stalin as great and constructive statesmen simply because they have succeeded in building up a great empire.[130]

The Anti-Imperialist Imperialism

The Bolshevik regime has won most of its adherents and sympathizers through the popular belief that it is anti-imperialistic. Soviet foreign policy is seen as aimed towards the liberation of peoples from colonial rule and its exploitations; the U.S.S.R. is esteemed particularly as a proponent of the national independence of Asiatic peoples. The Soviet Union insists, besides, that within its own frontiers, it has overcome tensions among the various national groups as well as the unjust, oppressive preponderance of the Great Russians.[131] All Soviet peoples, allegedly, live together in perfect harmony. The socialist common order does not burden them; on the contrary, it helps them.

This myth of the Soviet Union as a free community of equal peoples does not correspond to the facts. True, Lenin employed the slogan of the right of self-determination, including the right of secession from the Russian state, as a means of undermining the existing order in the fight against which his party had to gain power. To stress the difference from past regimes, the Bolsheviks fought what they called Great Russian chauvinism in the Ukraine, abolished russification measures, and favored the development of national consciousness and cultural life among the various peoples and nations living in the territories of the former Russian Empire under their control.[132] But this policy was only transitional. As the Soviet regime became more firmly established, centralizing tendencies started to grow despite federalistic facades. The Soviet Union constitution of 1924 replaced with a federation the former loose links among the various Soviet republics.[133] But the unifying and authoritative role of the central leadership of the Soviet Union Communist party was more and more asserted. The leadership of the Ukrainian Communist party was imposed by Moscow; Ukrainian nationalist and anti-Soviet deviations were uncovered. Obviously, the right of secession, mentioned also in the most recent Soviet constitution (the Stalin Constitution of 1936) is a pure fiction; it is self-evident that this right can never be implemented against the Soviet Union, the policies of whose leadership can never be directed against the interest of any nation. And in recent years there has been an increased tendency to identify Soviet leadership more or less with the Great Russian people, and to stress the positive aspects of the policies of Moscow and of the Tsars who built up the Russian empire. The Soviet Union appears as its heir which overcomes its shortcomings and evils.

Similar developments can be observed in the relations of the Soviet Communist party with the Communist parties outside the Soviet Union. The leadership of the Soviet party, established and realized in hidden forms during the existence of the Third International (dissolved in 1943), came into the open after World War II. This has been clearly shown in the conflict with Tito and his Communist party in Yugoslavia. When Tito rejected the advice — that is, the "orders," given him by the Soviet party—he was assailed as a traitor and excluded from the Communist community; and the Cominform (a bureau set up at the start of the cold war to coordinate actions of nine European Communist parties) turned against him.[134] All the discussions and political decisions of Communist parties take advantage of the formulas abstracted from the experience of the Soviet party. There are Trotskyites and Titoists everywhere; the history of the Soviet party is the authoritative textbook everywhere; and Lenin's and Stalin's works are classics everywhere.

Despite this concentration of the control of all national operations and policies as well as of all communist parties in the hands of the leaders of the U.S.S.R., despite organization of the economic policies and conduct of the foreign relations of the satellites according to the orders and interests of Moscow,[135] the assertion is made and upheld that the Soviet regime is anti-imperialistic. This claim is justified by the following dialectical artifice: imperialism means the exploitation of colonial territories in the interest of one class, the ruling class in the imperialist country; therefore, the policy of the Soviet Union cannot be imperialist, for there are no classes in the socialist Soviet Union, and all policies of the Soviet Union are policies of liberation from imperialist subjugation. It is not reality that determines the political concepts, but the concepts that determine reality. Therefore, Soviet imperialism, like the exploitation of satellite economies, appears as anti-imperialism, and the Soviet "anti-imperialism" becomes an important weapon against the influence of the West, including the United States. That this "anti-imperialism" is only a weapon of Soviet expansionism and imperialism (struggling to win powerful allies like the Chinese Communist People's Republic, or to undermine adversaries in the cold war — particularly by peace-talk) has not destroyed its propaganda value. The Soviet attack upon imperialism continues to attract many and to make Stalin's regime look like the greatest possible helper in the fight against European-American influence and controls, notably in Asia and the Middle East.

Bolshevism, Fascism, Nazism

The experiences and methods of Bolshevism have been used by anti-communist movements in the twentieth century. The conquest and maintenance of power by the Bolshevik minority has impressed and influenced anti-democratic and anti-liberal groups throughout Europe. A totalitarian regime — whose most striking features consist in the conquest and organization of unlimited controls by a strictly disciplined group with a secular political religion and claiming to express the will of the masses — proved realizable for the first time in the victory of Bolshevism.

Bolshevist methods could be taken over and imitated without accepting the contents of Marxism-Leninism. Totalitarian techniques of gaining and exercising power, totalitarian pressure and propaganda could be applied without using formulas and slogans determined by faith in the necessary coming of Communism. Totalitarian movements which fought the dominant liberal-democratic regimes in postwar Italy and in Germany of the Weimar Republic could exploit for themselves the nationalist emotionalism and the economic dissatisfaction of the masses. The masses disliked and resented not only the traditional-conservative elites but also their opponents, the democratic and socialist groups; for the democratic liberal opposition, when brought into power, was unable to establish a durable regime or to overcome its apparent association with defeat, as in Germany, or with disappointments about the fruits of victory, as in Italy.[136] The National Socialist and Fascist totalitarian movements (the fact that Italian Fascism used totalitarian features and oratory more for external display than for anything else is of no importance in this context) were able to appeal to the disappointments, frustrations and fears of those social groups, particularly the middle class and peasants, who by the loss of their property were likely to become proletarians. The lower classes resented this fate bitterly. For, contrary to Marxian predictions, they did not accept a proletarian-revolutionary class consciousness. Instead they joined movements promising them their old place in society and making the world meaningful by racial and nationalist myths. These myths could be sources of enthusiasm and of will to action, and could provide as well an explanation of all political and social catastrophes and riddles. These negative mysteries came forth as the conspiratorial work of evil forces and anti-social groups — which, for the Nazis, were the Jews, the eternal enemies of the Germanic-Nordic elite. The nationalist and racialist myth was able to defeat the Marxian pseudo-scientific myth of a necessary economically-determined development. The word socialism assumed a new meaning: it became the symbol of the operation against the traditional elites who regarded the authoritarian or capitalist order as something self-evident and natural;[137] whereas the new anti-Marxian movements appeared and acted as the spokesmen of the masses, integrating them into the national community, the racial *Volksgemeinschaft* of National Socialism. And the socialism expressed in these totalitarian movements claimed to be the voice of the so-called "young people" crying out against the old, decadent capitalist world.

The connection between Fascism and National Socialism on the one side and Bolshevism on the other was not often seen. This was the case, first, because the contents of the doctrine, the pseudo-religious dogmas, were different. Nationalism and racialism and Marxian internationalism seem to be worlds apart. Furthermore, Fascism and National Socialism emphasized from the beginning the central role of a person, the Duce or the Fuehrer; whereas the cult of Lenin (organized after his death) and of Stalin developed later, and had to be justified by making Lenin and Stalin the impersonal and superhuman representatives of the doctrine, great men in the sense of Hegelian philosophy in which the great men embody the movement and meaning of world history in their period. Finally, the similarity in the structure and in the methods of all totalitarian movements, the political religions of the twentieth century, was overlooked because Fascism and National Socialism appealed to traditional values and concepts, and tried to exploit traditional institutions like the Church and other conservative groups for their purposes. They disliked even the revolutionary phraseology of Bolshevism. Particularly, they insisted that they were the only efficient defenders against Communism and its threat of universal dissolution. It was not realized, or realized too late, that anti-Bolshevik totalitarianism is still a political secular religion to which everything is available as means of propaganda — in this case, the longing for a strong clear authority, the rescuing of national unity from the eternal strife of parties, and the hope of ending liberal-rationalist attacks against religion. If power is achieved, the conservative supporters are dropped and deprived of all independence, for what alone matters is the absolute power of *the* movement and its leadership. "The myth of the twentieth century," the doctrine of National Socialism, is just as intolerant and exclusive as the Marxian-Communist world outlook. Both mark the rise of an immanentism which makes all transcendent values and concepts merely instruments of the all-embracing power in this world.

This immanentism may be defined as a doctrine proclaiming

necessary development as the aim of life, as in Bolshevism, or as a myth glorifying the absolute domination of a racial elite, as in Nazism. It makes no difference; both forms elevate a political regime and its dominating group as ends in themselves. True, Bolshevism would show that its power is simply a means to the realization of perfect social justice by the classless society which makes full enjoyment of life possible for everyone; but in practice the means become the ends. What counts is the identification of the existence and power of the Soviet Union with work towards the goal: thereby, the totalitarian state of the Communist party determines what is just, good and meaningful. It becomes the present immanent "God." The identical, formal totalitarian structure proves more important than the divergent contents of National Socialist and Bolshevik doctrines.

What is the basis of these formal-structural identities? All totalitarian movements are political religions represented by a group, *the* party or *the* movement, with authority to interpret *the* only right and true doctrine. This strictly disciplined and organized group uses its absolute monopoly of propaganda and every other method of pressure to manage the masses — to harness their enthusiasm to create an artificial reality making an absurdity of any individual resistance. So the impression that no other world either exists or can exist is produced. That Fascism and National Socialism lack a doctrine purporting to show by scientific, economic-sociological analysis a necessary coming development of society and history, does not distinguish them essentially from Bolshevism. For Bolshevism the function of the doctrine is to put more and more power in the hands of the leaders, who can, as needed, adjust the doctrine.

Reasons for the World Success of Bolshevism

The success of Bolshevism is achieved by the utilization of the masses through a relatively small group of leaders. The leaders, at least at first, believe in the doctrine, and then, after seizure of power or long experience in the party, are interested primarily in organization and practical embodiment; the masses either do not actively support the old social order or regard prevailing conditions as intolerable and ripe for destruction. Bolshevism appears to these potentially or actually revolutionary masses as the negation of present conditions which must be overcome as a means of liberation from colonial rule or from the domination of estate owners. They believe that Bolshevism will create an ideal future with justice and without coercion. Bolshevik tactics and propaganda campaigns forever try to exploit widely various forms of discontent with the existing political and social regime so as to weaken real or potential adversaries, to undermine the resistance of the non-Bolshevik world and to bring the Communist party — signifying today the Soviet Union — finally into power. No sooner has the party reached power than it entrenches its totalitarian domination by applying systematic pressures and paralyzing tactical maneuvers to the non-Communists, some of whom are used as powerless partners in coalition governments. This system, submitting everything and everyone to its control, makes any organized public resistance impossible.

With appropriate variations in detail, this method was applied after the Second World War to the creation of satellite regimes in Eastern Europe.[138] The occupying Soviet armies, without resorting to an open use of force, helped to concentrate all power in the hands of the Communist minority. Even after their defeat in elections, the Hungarian Communists were backed by the Soviet forces. This compelled the non-Communist majorities in the government and in the parliament to decapitate themselves by excluding leaders and representatives whom the Reds deemed unreliable. Terrorist means, like the arrests of uncompromising politicians, helped to obtain and enforce subservient obedience. Soviet pressure transformed the minority into a majority, while the fear of the omnipresent Soviet power did not permit organized resistance. Public trials, like Cardinal Mindszenty's, were accompanied by assertions that a Church lending public support to the Communist government would be tolerated. Such policies helped to establish and entrench totalitarian control, for it was made crystal clear that any rebel would be crushed or forced to submit. Purges (like those of Gomolka in Poland, Rajk in Hungary, Kostov in Bulgaria, Slansky in Czechoslovakia) established within the various Communist parties the same insecurity that prevails in the Soviet party itself.

Satellite parties had to be completely dependent upon the Soviet masters in Moscow. That Tito and his Communist under-leaders could break away from Moscow control, after rejecting its demands, was possible only because the chief of Yugoslavia was not checked by a Soviet army of occupation. He dared to face the threat of pressure from outside and turned his totalitarian machinery against Moscow and its friends. The conquest of power in European countries outside the sphere of Soviet armies and direct Soviet influence failed because the Communist parties, even when accepted as members of the ruling coalitions, were not strong enough to use their government positions to subjugate the non-Communist parties step by step. These parties, after a transitional period, were therefore able to oppose Communists and finally to expel them from the cabinets. Such operations were successfully performed not only in France and Italy with their strong Communist organizations[139]— where a Communist coup d'etat backed by Soviet intervention would have meant a new world war — but even in Finland, where the U.S.S.R. was not willing to intervene when the Communists lost control of the police. It was only in China that the direct menace of a Soviet army was not required for the victory of the Communists though occupation of Manchuria by the Red Army was very helpful. It provided an opportunity for the Chinese Reds to receive the weapons of the defeated Japanese armies. Therefore, Red China's relations with Moscow are quite different from those of the satellites. In spite of this, Mao Tse-tung's regime regards Leninism as its official doctrine, uses Soviet technicians and Soviet economic aid and is dependent upon Soviet arms for the war in Korea.

The Bolshevik leaders, after their seizure of power in Russia, had expected a quite different development. They believed that revolutions in countries industrially and technically more advanced, particularly Germany, would immediately follow the signal of the October revolution. But the Russian example was not imitated; the Soviet republics in Hungary and Munich proved shortlived and unimportant. But although hopes for seizure of power by Communists outside the Soviet frontiers, and the incessant work of the Third International for this goal proved to be futile until World War II,[140] Bolshevism attained extraordinary successes in other ways than that of the seizure of government. Communist parties came into being everywhere; they attracted the radical intelligentsia, appearing as the instruments needed to realize a progressive social order. The Soviet mythology proved indestructible. Disappointed Communists who left the party were replaced by new believers and sympathizers. Disappointed in their turn, they too were destined to repeat the accusations of their predecessors after a few years, when they had abandoned the "God that failed" and had become enemies of the system and the politico-social creed which had so bitterly disappointed them. A most impressive proof of the tenacity of Soviet mythology is its having survived all attacks of ex-Communists: from Reuter (the secretary general of the Communist party who is, today, as mayor of Berlin, a most zealous fighter against Soviet expansionism) to Ruth Fischer; from Souvarine (the former member of the Presidium of the Third International who later wrote a devastating description of Stalin's policies) to Doriot; from Gitlow to Whittaker Chambers.

There were highs and lows in the attraction exercised by the Soviet mythology. Stalin did not care primarily to win over intellectuals. The changes in Soviet policies took place with very little consideration for the feelings of the pro-Communist fellow-travellers or even of the various national communist parties. The power politics of the Soviet Union mattered first, while the surprise and indignation of those admirers of the Soviet Union, and of foreign Communists, who were shocked by the agreement with Nazi Germany in 1939, were disregarded. What mattered much more was the establishment of "apparatchiki" abroad, of men and women who were willing simply to take any order from Moscow, to accept any political line of the Kremlin, to believe in it without hesitation, and to carry it out with enthusiastic obedience. The purges in foreign parties served to educate and to nurture these "apparatchiki" with their absolute loyalty to the Stalinist masters. This process is called

95

"bolshevization." [141]   All Communists in the world are supposed to realize (in theory as well as in practice) that the leadership of the Soviet Union and its party is the world leadership, that its policies are not the policies of one government, of one party, but the policies of the fatherland of all Communists and of all progressive mankind.

The emphasis upon the "apparatchiki," the true Bolsheviks, who master all the techniques and means necessary for conspiracy as well as for the leadership of legal parties (often by hidden control) does not, of course, exclude interest in Communist mass movements and in the confusion of public opinion. All possibilities for exercising pressure in the interest of Soviet policies — by control of unions, by strikes, by parliamentary maneuvers, by exploiting antiwar feelings of the masses and of more or less gullible intellectuals — must be carefully utilized. Legal and illegal means do not exclude each other. The "apparatchik" conspirator is helped by mass movements and by signers of petitions and appeals, like the Stockholm appeal, which he organizes. Any means to win followers and conscious or unconscious sympathizers on the one side, and to cause insecurity, confusion and disintegration on the other, is applied. The same Communists (who, once in power, will establish totalitarian control) now take advantage themselves of legal guarantees. They would use German nationalism for their purposes and at the same time defend the Oder-Neisse frontier which is unfavorable to Germany. The Bolshevik propaganda would try to impress the masses, especially those of Asia, which oppose foreign influences and regard the Soviet Union as the anti-imperialist fighter for the improvement of living conditions; simultaneously it would appeal to intellectuals, who (like the Webbs in their old age) admire the grandiose schemes of Soviet planning and organization.

The existence and strength of the Soviet Union are crucial for world revolutionary endeavors. This became clear during the Brest-Litovsk crisis of 1918 when Lenin refused to sacrifice the Soviet regime to utopian hopes for an immediate world revolution — a policy which would only have aided German power politics in wiping out the Soviet regime. This was also the meaning of Stalin's famous sentence about the need to realize socialism in one country, the Soviet Union of course. Stalin did not surrender his expectation of revolutions outside the U.S.S.R.[142] The power of the Soviet Union is designed to help the world revolution. Trotsky, Stalin's outmaneuvered and defeated competitor for Lenin's heritage, had accentuated the realization of the revolutionary process by the proletariat of all countries, in his formula about the permanent revolution. Today all Communist parties are coordinated with the foreign policy of the Soviet Union. With the dissolution of the Third International the pretense that there is a Communist institutional world authority above the Soviet Communist party has vanished. The Cominform is only a secretariat relaying Moscow's orders. The chances of world revolution are identical with chances for the expansion of Moscow's power.

Up to now all Communist movements opposed to Stalin's policies and control have remained — like the Trotskyite attempts to establish a Fourth International — unimportant sectarian affairs. Even today one may venture to state that Tito's anti-Stalinist Yugoslav Communism will not serve as an attractive example for the rise of similar movements among Communists of other countries. This, of course, does not diminish the importance of Yugoslavia's defection.

Despite the equation of Bolshevism-Communism with the Soviet Union in our time, it is necessary to regard Bolshevism as a movement of world importance, transcending the reality of power politics and conflicts among superpowers and their followers. Bolshevism is a conscious and planned attempt to form the whole of existence in accordance with a belief that men are only parts in the self-sufficient perpetual society-machine of *this* world. Under Communism each individual will reach the fullest social conscience. There will no longer be any contradiction between private and public interests. But in the reality of the Bolshevik experiment only one consideration prevails: What is useful and necessary for the rule of those who dominate in the name of the coming perfect classless society? The power of those who plan and work for the necessarily coming order of the future becomes an end in itself; the realization of the promised aim is more and more delayed, or postponed to a future farther and farther away.

Bolshevik effort is based upon the assumption of a limitless perfectibility of man, his capacity to know the over-all character of coming history and society and to use this knowledge for the construction of the future era. It brings about a present reality in which man and society are only means and material for the social engineer. Utopia, resting on a rationalist-scientific knowledge proffering absolute liberty by a collectivist system, creates a totalitarian control by the party directing the present collectivist experiment. This control summons to itself modern technical means and methods of domination and can, therefore, become more omnipotent and more engulfing than any previous tyranny. Utopia becomes an ideology, serving only to warrant the actions of the totalitarian masters and absolutely unconnected with the brutal nature of reality.

This ideology has great influence: first, because it is backed by the experience of the successful conquest of a great empire; second, because it justifies the shifting of the means to accord with the power situation (only centralizing tendencies and the will to exercise a constant totalitarian control remain unchanged) ; and finally, because this ideology is grasped by many not in its eeffects but only in its promises. These promises make the existing conditions look darker than they really are; and the myth of Bolshevism is compared with the imperfect reality, which causes longing as well as suffering. Such a myth expresses basic tendencies in a secularized world. For its elements are these: belief in necessary development towards a perfect order here on earth which will function without a specific directing group;[143] belief in the unlimited effects of education and alterations in economics and social organization; belief in complete mastery of society by men who know the laws of social structure and development; and belief that mysteries can be eliminated from public life, since they are only proofs of an insufficient knowledge which can be overcome. These tendencies are expressed by Bolshevism in a very simple system which explains, at the same time, the means by which the perfect society can and will be reached. The system, despite its drastic action in the present imperfect world, is based on ultra-optimistic expectations for the future. In the name of the coming perfection everything which promotes its coming is permitted. Utopianism is a powerful source of clear, simple faith in the future of mankind. All alternatives are rejected as the products of obscurantist superstition, of the will to defend an egoistic and obsolete class rule, as expressions. of decadent pessimism, relativism, agnosticism, and nihilism.

Intellectuals are attracted by this political secular religion because it gives them certainty and goals for activity. And the masses are seduced by its role as the destroyer of injustices and imperfections. The intellectuals do not realize that the Bolshevik certainty is based on the whim of brutal power politicians who interpret the doctrine according to the needs of totalitarian control; and the masses are unaware that Bolshevism, when victorious, replaces existing imperfections by a system of totalitarian domination — a system infinitely worse than the very imperfect conditions of the present. Yet it would impose upon its victims an artificial reality depriving them of the power to evaluate the actuality of existence. Everything is done to make the regime seem omnipotent as well as inevitable, to make its "necessity" seem to be "freedom."

CONCLUSION

Bolshevism has one of its roots in the West. The starting point and basis of its doctrine, Marxism, has been described by one of its two creators, Friedrich Engels, as the offspring of German philosophy, English economics and French sociology (utopian socialism). Marxism became Bolshevism — a movement to change the world — in Russia owing to the activities of Lenin. He embraced Marxism as a belief. He took it seriously as a guide to action, as a tool to effectuate a total, permanent revolution, and not merely, like the Western or Westernized moderate socialists, as a justification for social and political reforms which would be steps in a slow process of peaceful humanitarian evolution.

Lenin was the product and the nemesis of the Russian radical intelligentsia. He shared its belief that Western socialist and progressive doctrines were absolute truth and a secular religion regulating all of life; but he overcame its unfitness for continuous and systematic practical action. After accumulating experience in methods of organization and struggle for power as leader of a socialist group, the Bolshevik faction of the Social Democratic party, he exploited boldly the unexpected breakdown of Tsarism. His party took over, established the Soviet regime, and, by building up its totalitarian power, "the socialism in one country" of Stalin, became identified with the world revolution. The disciples of the West grew to despise the West, which, in its decadence, did not dare to make socialism into a reality. They exploited, without hesitation or pity, the tears, sweat and longing of the Soviet masses, deceiving them and flattering them, to construct a new world without capitalists. This red empire is dominated by a leadership monopolizing all political, economic, cultural, and ideological controls. These imitators of the West, whose faith had come from the West, became, because of successful power politics, men sitting in judgment upon the West, asking its submission to Soviet policies and methods, while threatening it with conquest and destruction. They face a world often uncertain about its own traditions, longing for security at any price and exhausted by internal conflicts.

101

In this tired world beliefs have often become ideologies reflecting and justifying egoistic power and enervated traditions. Too much brutality shrewdly implemented is opposed by too much sophistication inclined to despair about itself, though it has not yet completely lost the memories of its great origins and the will to survive. This power conflict would have been settled in favor of the paralyzing Soviet strength, exploiting the prostration that followed World War II, if the European West had not the support of the United States. The technical, industrial, and economic means at the disposal of Washington forced Moscow to be cautious in the use of revolutionary situations and to replace open conquest by the methods of cold war. There is every reason to expect that world conquest by the fatherland of world revolution, the Soviet Communism, will not happen, despite the success of its ally in China. There is even reason for hope that this containment may be achieved without an atomic world war.

Bolshevism is surely a political and military problem, but at the same time much more than that: it is an accusation against the imperfections and errors of its opponents; it thrives on these errors and imperfections. It brings into the open and develops to fullest size an immanentist secularism (viewing the attainment of a perfectly-functioning society with maximum satisfactions available to everyone through social engineering as the aim of the very existence of men and their society). All mysteries — it is promised by Bolshevism — will disappear. They will be reduced to socially useful forces: adoration of God replaced by relentless and enthusiastic work towards the classless society; contemplation replaced by meaningful labor — with, of course, organized hours of rest and leisure; and all experience lowered to the level of problems of social science, management, organization, and administration.

Against a tired and skeptical immanentism Bolshevism sets up an appeal to an all-embracing, self-confident and courageous one. Bolshevism raises not only political economic and military issues but also moral and religious ones. Therefore, power is necessary to overcome this danger, but its use alone is not sufficient. Even after the downfall of its Soviet form it could survive, since totalitarianism is not exclusively bound to Marxism, although Marxism has provided the doctrinal background, the dogmatic ("scientific") formulas for its most efficient form to date.

The fundamental problem of our time is expressed in these questions: Is not something wrong with the assumption that social perfection here on earth is possible? Does not this assumption, if taken seriously as a guide for practical action, result in less rather than in more perfection? Have not the "last wars," for instance, fought in order to abolish war itself, resulted in more rather than fewer violent wars? Has not the Bolshevik utopia of the withering away of the state led only to the establishment of totalitarian rule?

Perfection is utopianism; and utopianism taken seriously — as it was taken by Lenin and the Bolsheviks — must result in tyranny; for its forces attempt to substitute an imposed artificial world for the reality of creation. The Bolshevist utopian faith in the unlimited power of man as builder of a perfect self-sufficient world must be overcome by the moderate conception of man's limited power. Man's nature is not a self-sufficient one; man is a being between the angels and the animals, faced with the necessity of making choices among evils and imperfections, selecting the lesser ones. Man is inexorably bound to various traditions and environments; his history is neither a straight nor a winding dialectical way to more and more perfection, ending here on earth in the absolute self-sufficient perfection of a classless society. Perfectionist utopianism, of which Bolshevism represents a most efficient variety, is the greatest danger of our time. It may result in a fierce activism — as in Soviet Communism — or a cynical relativism: since this perfection cannot be achieved, everything is equally wrong, because equally imperfect. Then everything becomes a problem of power politics. Thus arises a terrible prospect: the choice between totalitarian control based upon a denial of reality by a wrong and perverse utopia and a garrison state, guaranteeing perhaps a more secure life and more variety for the individual, but defending the existing conditions without any quest for spiritual and intellectual foundations.

Anti-Bolshevism is not enough,[144] for it selects the battlefield according to the dictates of Bolshevism. The prison built by the Bolshevik belief in the self-sufficiency of society in this world must be demolished. The real world of human imperfections must be discovered again. True freedom consists not in the necessity of a coming classless society, but in the capacity to produce an infinite variety of men and human groups embodying history and society, expressing and emphasizing the manifold aspects of human nature. Common to all kinds of historical life is recognition by human endeavor of an order which cannot be exhausted in a particular form arising in time; only such recognition can be the basis of human freedom. It is the negative merit of Bolshevism to have challenged this conception of human nature; and its challenge can only be answered by our becoming aware of its fundamentals.

For Bolshevism, the aim of historical development is to remove all mystery, to make men total masters of society. This conception is opposed to the view that the aim of history cannot be itself an historical form. The Christian will add that the center and aim of history is the Cross and the City of God, not the prolongation of human time but its fulfillment, transformation and elevation.

All rejections of the basic faith and doctrine of Bolshevism do not save us from the question: Why did this error, this misconception of man and society, this utopian evolutionism, appear attractive to so many? Here is a concrete challenge — the challenge to complacency about the existing order. Surely Bolshevism has replaced or would replace it by a much worse order — by a totalitarian tyranny fostering lies, corruption, cruelty, and inhumanity. There would be no chance left to fight for improvement and for more social justice; instead every opportunity for vicious and evil action would be tremendously increased. Nevertheless, Bolshevism, its rise and its successes, ought to stir us to meditate about what is unsatisfactory in the present world and about what has caused many, erroneously, of course, to accept Bolshevism as the answer to our demands for the better realization of social justice and human rights. That Bolshevism could develop into a world danger is surely an accusation against the non-Bolshevist world.

CONCLUSION

It is not sufficient (though required) to prevent it from spreading by external means; it is necessary to find its roots in our society.

Therefore, the Bolshevist disease and evil can have good and happy results. For it may force us to reflect upon the foundations of our existence and social order. The same movement which denies the conscience of men and replaces belief in social reform by a doctrine of necessary development can become a means of sharpening our social conscience and effectuating social and political reforms. Bolshevism's mobilization of the masses and of the world would then, against its own will and doctrine, help to bring about real progress and improvement. The importance of the Soviet regime would be a negative one; that is, it would serve as a most striking refutation of the claims and pretenses in whose name it began. The great experiment of the Soviet Union, precisely through its lies and its failure, would help us to grasp the truth. Even a lie and a failure can be compelled to serve the right order. The blackest tragedies and the most depressing catastrophes of history have their positive function and meaning.

DOCUMENTS AND SOURCE MATERIAL*

I. *Fundamentals of Marxism-Leninism*

1) Dialectical Materialism

. . . the genius of Marx consists precisely in the fact that he furnished answers to questions which had already engrossed the foremost minds of humanity.

The Marxian doctrine is omnipotent because it is true. It is complete and harmonious, and provides men with an integral world conception which is irreconcilable with any form of superstition, reaction, or defence of bourgeois oppression. It is the legitimate successor of the best that was created by humanity in the nineteenth century in the shape of German philosophy, English political economy and French Socialism.

> V. I. Lenin, "The Three Sources and Three Component Parts of Marxism," *Selected Works,* Vol. XI, London, 1939, p. 3.

The philosophy of Marxism is materialism. . . . But Marx did not stop at the materialism of the eighteenth century; he advanced philosophy. He enriched it with the acquisitions of German classical philosophy, especially of Feuerbach. The chief of these acquisitions is dialectics, i.e., the doctrine of development in its fullest and deepest form, free of one-sidedness — the doctrine of the relativity of human knowledge, which provides us with a reflection of eternally developing matter. The latest discoveries of natural science — radium, electrons, the transmutation of elements — have remarkably confirmed Marx's dialectical materialism, despite the

---

* Permission to quote from SELECTED WORKS OF LENIN was granted by the publishers, Lawrence & Wishart, Ltd., 81 Chancery Lane, London, W.C. 1, England.

The Editors of THE CURRENT DIGEST OF THE SOVIET PRESS in New York, N. Y.—an indispensable tool for all students of Bolshevism—consented to the reproduction of material published by them.

Dr. Michael Pap, research assistant to the Committee on International Relations, of the University of Notre Dame, Notre Dame, Indiana, translated the quotations from the Russian books and periodicals.

teachings of the bourgeois philosophers with their "new" reversions to old and rotten idealism.

Deepening and developing philosophical materialism, Marx completed it, extended its knowledge of nature to the knowledge of human society. Marx's historical materialism was one of the greatest achievements of scientific thought. The chaos and arbitrariness that had previously reigned in the views on history and politics gave way to a strikingly integral and harmonious scientific theory, which shows how, in consequence of the growth of productive forces, out of one system of social life another and higher system develops — how capitalism, for instance, grows out of feudalism.

Just as man's knowledge reflects nature (i.e., developing matter), which exists independently of him, so man's knowledge (i.e., the various views and doctrines — philosophical, religious, political and so forth) reflects the economic system of society. Political institutions are a superstructure on the economic foundation. We see, for example, that the various political forms of the modern European states serve to fortify the rule of the bourgeoisie over the proletariat.

> *Ibid.,* pp. 4-5.

"To Hegel . . . ," wrote Marx, "the process of thinking, which, under the name of 'the Idea,' he even transforms into an independent subject, is the demiurgos (the creator, the maker) of the real world. . . . With me, on the contrary, the idea is nothing else than the material world reflected by the human mind, and translated into forms of thought."

> *Ibid.,* p. 14, "Karl Marx." Cf. *Capital,* Vol. I, Edition of Charles H. Kerr & Co., Chicago, Preface to the Second Edition.

. . . according to Marx, dialectics is "the science of the general laws of motion—both of the external world and of human thought." (Ludwig Feuerbach)

This revolutionary side of Hegel's philosophy was adopted and developed by Marx. Dialectical materialism "no longer needs any philosophy standing above the other sciences." (Cf. F. Engels, *Anti-Dühring*) Of former philosophy there remains "the science of thought and its laws — formal logic and dialectics." (Cf. *Anti-*

Dühring) And dialectics, as understood by Marx, and in conformity with Hegel, includes what is now called the theory of knowledge, or epistemology. . . .

Ibid., p. 17.

. . . this idea (of development) is far more comprehensive, far richer in content than the current idea of evolution. A development that seemingly repeats the stages already passed, but repeats them otherwise, on a higher basis ("negation of negation"), a development, so to speak, in spirals, not in a straight line;— a development by leaps, catastrophes, revolutions;—"breaks in continuity"; — the transformation of quantity into quality;— the inner impulses to development, imparted by the contradiction and conflict of the various forces and tendencies acting on a given body, or within a given phenomenon, or within a given society;— the interdependence of the closest, indissoluble connection of all sides of every phenomenon (while history constantly discloses ever new sides), a connection that provides a uniform, law-governed, universal process of motion — such are some of the features of dialectics as a richer (than the ordinary) doctrine of development.

Ibid., pp. 17-18.

Hegelian dialectics, as the most comprehensive, the most rich in content, and the most profound doctrine of development, was regarded by Marx and Engels as the greatest achievement of classical German philosophy. They considered every other formulation of the principle of development, of evolution, one-sided and poor in content, and distorting and mutilating the real course of development (often proceeding by leaps, catastrophes and revolutions) in nature and in society.

Ibid., p. 16.

"The real unity of the world consists in its materiality, and this is proved . . . by a long and tedious development of philosophy and natural science. . . ." "Motion is the mode of existence of matter. Never anywhere has there been matter without motion, nor can there be. . . . But if the . . . question is raised: what then are

109

thought and consciousness, and whence they come, it becomes apparent that they are products of the human brain and that man himself is a product of nature, which has been developed in and along with its environment; whence it is self-evident that the products of the human brain, being in the last analysis also products of nature, do not contradict the rest of nature but are in correspondence with it."

> *Ibid.,* p. 14, quoting from F. Engels, *Herr Eugen Dühring's Revolution in Science (Anti-Dühring)*, English edition, 1934, pp. 44-45.

"The great basic question of all philosophy, especially of modern philosophy, is that concerning the relation of thinking and being ... spirit to nature ... which is primary, spirit or nature. . . . The answers which the philosophers gave to this question split them into two great camps. Those who asserted the primacy of spirit to nature and, therefore, in the last instance, assumed world creation in some form or other . . . comprised the camp of idealism. The others, who regarded nature as primary, belong to the various schools of materialism." (Cf. F. Engels, *Ludwig Feuerbach,* English edition, 1934, pp. 30-31)

Any other use of the concepts of (philosophical) idealism and materialism leads only to confusion. Marx decidedly rejected not only idealism, always connected in one way or another with religion, but also the views, especially widespread in our day, of Hume and Kant, agnosticism, criticism, positivism in their various forms, regarding such a philosophy as a "reactionary" concession to idealism. . . .

> *Ibid.,* p. 15.

2)   The Historical Process

. . . history discloses a struggle between nations and societies as well as within nations and societies, and, in addition, an alternation of periods of revolution and reaction, peace and war, stagnation and rapid progress or decline are facts that are generally known. Marxism provided the clue which enables us to discover the laws governing this seeming labyrinth and chaos, namely, the theory of the class struggle.

110

"The history of all hitherto existing society is the history of class struggles," wrote Marx in the *Communist Manifesto*.

> V. I. Lenin, "Karl Marx," *Selected Works*, Vol. XI, London, 1939, p. 20.

The theory of the class struggle was not created by Marx, but by the bourgeoisie before Marx, and generally speaking it is acceptable to the bourgeoisie. A Marxist is one who extends the acceptance of the class struggle to the acceptance of the dictatorship of the proletariat.

> V. I. Lenin, "The State and Revolution," *Selected Works*, Vol. VII, p. 33.

"Our epoch, the epoch of the bourgeoisie . . . has simplified the class antagonisms. Society as a whole is more and more splitting up into two great hostile camps, into two great classes directly facing each other — bourgeoisie and proletariat."

> V. I. Lenin, "Karl Marx," *Selected Works*, Vol. XI, p. 21, quoting Communist Manifesto.

"Of all the classes that stand face to face with the bourgeoisie today, the proletariat alone is a really revolutionary class. The other classes decay and finally disappear in the face of modern industry; the proletariat is its special and essential product."

"The lower middle class, the small manufacturer, the shopkeeper, the artisan, the peasant, all these fight against the bourgeoisie to save from extinction their existence as fractions of the lower middle class. They are therefore not revolutionary, but conservative. Nay more, they are reactionary, for they try to roll back the wheel of history. If by chance they are revolutionary, they are so only in view of their impending transfer into the proletariat; they thus defend not their present, but their future intents; they desert their own standpoint to place themselves at that of the proletariat."

> *Ibid.*, p. 21, quoting *Communist Manifesto*.

. . . Marx deduces the inevitability of the transformation of capitalist society into socialist society wholly and exclusively from the economic law of motion of contemporary society. The socialization of labor, which is advancing ever more rapidly in thousands of forms, and which has manifested itself very strikingly during the half-century that has elapsed since the death of Marx in the growth of large scale production, capitalist cartels, syndicates and trusts, as well as in the gigantic increase in the dimensions, and power of finance capital, forms the chief material foundation for the inevitable coming of Socialism. The intellectual and moral driving force and the physical executant of this transformation is the proletariat, which is trained by capitalism itself. The struggle of the proletariat, against the bourgeoisie, which manifests itself in various and, as to its content, increasingly richer forms, inevitably becomes a political struggle aiming at the conquest of political power by the proletariat ("the dictatorship of the proletariat"). The socialization of production is bound to lead to the conversion of the means of production into the property of society, to the "expropriation of the expropriators." This conversion will directly result in an immense increase in productivity of labour, a reduction of working hours, and the replacement of the remnants, the ruins of small-scale primitive, disunited production by collective and improved labor.

Ibid., pp. 33-34.

Marx defined the fundamental task of proletarian tactics in strict conformity with all the postulates of his materialist-dialectical conception. Only an objective consideration of the sum total of reciprocal relations of all the classes of a given society without exception, and consequently, a consideration of the objective stage of development of that society and of the reciprocal relations between it and other societies, can serve as a basis for the correct tactics of the advanced class. At the same time, all classes and all countries are not regarded statistically, but dynamically, i.e., not in a state of immobility, but in motion (the laws of which are determined by the economic conditions of existence of each class). Motion, in its turn, is regarded not only from the standpoint of the past, but also from the standpoint of the future, and, at the same time, not in accordance with the vulgar conception of the "evolutionists," who

112

see only slow changes, but dialectically: in historical developments of such magnitude twenty years are no more than a day, Marx wrote to Engels, "although later there may come days in which twenty years are concentrated" (*Briefwechsel*, Vol. III, p. 127). At each stage of development, at each moment, proletarian tactics must take account of this objectively inevitable dialectics of human history, on the one hand utilising the periods of political stagnation or of sluggish, so-called "peaceful" development in order to develop the class-consciousness, strength and fighting capacity of the advanced class, and, on the other hand, conducting all this work of utilisation towards the "final aim" of the movement of the advanced class and towards the creation in it of the faculty for practically performing great tasks in the great days in which "twenty years are concentrated."

Ibid., pp. 37-38.

3. State and Dictatorship of the Proletariat

The state is the product and the manifestation of the irreconcilability of class antagonisms. The state arises when, where and to the extent that class antagonisms cannot be objectively reconciled. And, conversely, the existence of the state proves that the class antagonisms are irreconcilable.

V. I. Lenin, "The State and Revolution," *Selected Works*, Vol. VII, London, 1937, p. 8.

. . . if the state is the product of irreconcilable class antagonisms, if it is a power standing above society and "increasingly alienating itself from it," it is clear that the liberation of the oppressed class is impossible, not only without a violent revolution, but also without the destruction of the apparatus of state power which was created by the ruling class. . . .

Ibid., p. 10.

A democratic republic is the best possible political shell for capitalism, and, therefore, once capital has gained control of this very best shell, it establishes its power so securely, so firmly, that no

change, either of persons, of institutions, or of parties in the bour-
geois-democratic republic, can shake it.

Ibid., p. 15.

The petty-bourgeois democrats, democrats, such as our Socialist-
Revolutionaries and Mensheviks, and also their twin brothers, the
social-chauvinists and opportunists of Western Europe, all expect
"more" from universal suffrage. They themselves share and instil
into the minds of the people the wrong idea that universal suffrage
"in the modern state" is really capable of expressing the will of the
majority of the toilers and of ensuring its realization.

Ibid., p. 15.

. . . the doctrine of Marx and Engels concerning the inevitability
of a violent revolution refers to the bourgeois state. The latter
cannot be superseded by the proletarian state (the dictatorship of
the proletariat) in the process of "withering away;" as a general
rule, this can happen only by means of a violent revolution.

Ibid., p. 21.

The state is a special organization of force; it is the organization of
violence for the suppression of some class. What class must the proletariat suppress? Naturally, only the exploiting class, i.e., the bourgeoisie. The toilers need a state only to overcome the resistance of
the exploiters, and only the proletariat can direct this suppression,
carry it out; . . .

Ibid., p. 24.

By educating the workers' party, Marxism educates the vanguard
of the proletariat which is capable of assuming power and of leading the whole people to socialism, of directing and organizing the
new order, of being the teacher, guide and leader of all the toiling
and exploited in the task of building up their social life without the
bourgeoisie and against the bourgeoisie.

Ibid., p. 26.

"Between capitalist and communist society lies the period of the revolutionary transformation of the one into the other. There corresponds to this also a political transition period in which the state can be nothing but the revolutionary dictatorship of the proletariat."

Ibid., p. 78, quoting Marx: "Critique of the Gotha Programme."

. . . democracy itself begins to wither away owing to the simple fact that, freed from capitalist slavery, from the untold horrors, savagery, absurdities and infamies of capitalist exploitation, people will gradually become accustomed to observing the elementary rules of social life that have been known for centuries and repeated for thousands of years in all copy-book maxims; they will become accustomed to observing them without force, without compulsion, without subordination, without the special apparatus for compulsion which is called the state.

Ibid., p. 81.

"In a higher phase of communist society after the enslaving subordination of individuals under division of labour, and therewith also the antithesis between mental and physical labour, has vanished; after labour has become not merely a means to live but has become itself the primary necessity of life; after the productive forces have also increased with the all-around development of the individual, and all the springs of co-operative wealth flow more abundantly — only then can the narrow horizon of bourgeois right be fully left behind and society inscribe on its banners: from each according to his ability, to each according to his needs!"

Ibid., p. 87, quoting Marx: "Critique of the Gotha Programme."

. . . Kautsky accidentally stumbled upon one true idea (namely, that dictatorship is power unrestricted by any laws) but he failed to give a definition of dictatorship. . . .

V. I. Lenin, "The Proletarian Revolution and the Renegade Kautsky," *Selected Works,* Vol. VII, p. 122.

During the epoch of the dictatorship of the proletariat there can be no policy of universal freedom in our country, i.e., no freedom of speech, press, etc., for the bourgeoisie. Our domestic policy reduces itself to granting a maximum of freedom to the proletarian strata in town and country, in denying even a minimum of freedom to the remnants of the bourgeois class. This constitutes the crux of our policy, based on the dictatorship of the proletariat.

J. Stalin, *Leninism*, I, New York, 1943, pp. 41-42.

. . . The dictatorship of the proletariat is the weapon of the proletarian revolution, its origin, its most important stronghold which is called into being, first, to crush the resistance of the overthrown exploiters, and to consolidate its achievements; secondly, to lead the proletarian revolution to its completion, to lead the revolution onward to the complete victory of socialism.

. . . the important thing is to retain power, to consolidate it and make it invincible. What is required to attain this end? At least three main tasks confronting the dictatorship of the proletariat "on the morrow" of victory must be fulfilled. They are: a) to break the resistance of the landlords and capitalists overthrown and expropriated by the revolution, and to liquidate every attempt they make to restore the power of capital; b) to organize construction in such a way as will rally all toilers around the proletariat and to carry on this work in such a way as will prepare for the liquidation, the extinction of classes; c) to arm the revolution and to organise the army of the revolution for the struggle against the external enemy and for the struggle against imperialism.

J. Stalin, *Leninism*, I, New York, 1934, pp. 41-42; *Sotchinenia*, Vol. VI, Moscow, 1947, pp. 108 f.

Marxism-Leninism teaches that the violent overthrow of the domination of the exploiting classes and establishment of the dictatorship of the proletariat is a general law of the Socialist Revolution. Only the working class, guided by a Marxist-Leninist party, is capable of leading and carrying through to the finish the class struggle against the exploiters. . . . The recognition of the necessity of carrying through the class struggle to the dictatorship of the proletariat is the cornerstone of the Marxist-Leninist theory of transformation of capitalist society into Socialist society. Marxism-Leninism is incompatible with opportunistic ideas to the effect that the transition from capitalism to Socialism can be carried out peacefully on the basis of parliamentary voting. . . . Democratic institutions in the capitalist countries are only a screen for the dictatorship of the bourgeoisie. No elections and no parliament can tear power from the bourgeoisie and liquidate the domination of capital. . . . The Right Socialists who say that capitalist slavery can be eliminated in parliamentary fashion merely protect the dictatorship of the bourgeoisie from its violent overthrow by the proletariat.

P. Fedoseev, "The Marxist Theory of Class and Class Struggle," *Bolshevik,* Moscow, July 1948, No. 14, p. 69.

4) Imperialism

Imperialism is capitalism in that stage of development in which the domination of monopolies and finance capital has established itself; in which the export of capital has acquired pronounced importance; in which the division of the world among the international trusts has begun; in which the partition of all the territories of the globe among the great capitalist powers has been completed.

V. I. Lenin, "Imperialism, the Highest Stage of Capitalism," *Selected Works,* Vol. V, London, 1936, p. 81.

The characteristic features of imperialism is precisely that it strives to annex not only agricultural regions, but even highly industrialised regions (German appetite for Belgium; French appetite for Lorraine), because 1) the fact that the world is already partitioned obliges those contemplating a new partition to stretch out their hands to any kind of territory, and 2) because an essential feature of imperialism is the rivalry between a number of great powers in the striving for hegemony, i.e., for the conquest of territory, not so much directly for themselves as to weaken the adversary and undermine his hegemony.

Ibid., pp. 83-84.

The European war, which the governments and the bourgeois parties of all countries have been preparing for decades, has broken out. The growth of armaments, the extreme sharpening of the struggle for markets in the epoch of the latest, the imperialist, stage in the development of capitalism in the foremost countries and the dynastic interests of the most backward East European monarchies were inevitably bound to bring about, and have brought about, the present war. To seize land and to conquer foreign nations, to ruin a competing nation and to pillage her wealth, to divert the attention of the toiling masses from the internal political crises of Russia, Germany, England and other countries, to disunite the workers and fool them with nationalism, to exterminate their vanguard in order to weaken the revolutionary movement of the proletariat — such is the only real content, the significance and the meaning of the present war.

Ibid., p. 123

Under present conditions, it is impossible to determine, from the standpoint of the international proletariat, whether the defeat of one or the other group of belligerent nations is the lesser evil for socialism. For us Russian Social-Democrats, however, there cannot be the slightest doubt that, from the standpoint of the working class and of the toiling masses of all nations of Russia, the lesser evil would be the defeat of the tsarist monarchy, of the most reactionary and barbarous government that is oppressing the greatest number of nations and the largest mass of the population of Europe and Asia.

Ibid., p. 129.

Imperialism, i.e., monopoly capitalism, which finally matured only in the twentieth century, is, by virtue of its fundamental economic traits, distinguished by the least attachment to peace and freedom, and by the greatest and universal development of militarism everywhere.

V. I. Lenin, "Proletarian Revolution and Renegade Kautsky," *Selected Works,* Vol. VII, pp. 125-126.

Leninism is Marxism in the epoch of imperialism and of the proletarian revolution. . . . Marx and Engels lived and worked in the pre-revolutionary epoch (we have the proletarian revolution in mind) when developed imperialism did not yet exist, in the period of preparation of the proletarians for the revolution was not yet a direct, practical inevitability. Lenin, the disciple of Marx and Engels, lived and worked in the epoch of developed imperialism.

Stalin, *Leninism,* I, p. 14; *Sotchinenia,* Vol. VI, Moscow, 1947, p. 71.

Imperialism denotes the omnipotence of the monopolist trusts and syndicates, of the banks and of the financial oligarchy in the industrial countries. In the fight against this omnipotence, the customary methods of the working class — trade unions and co-operative organisations, parliamentary parties and parliamentary struggle — proved quite inadequate. Either place yourself at the mercy of capital, linger in misery as of old and sink lower and lower, or adopt a new weapon — this is the alternative imperialism puts before the vast masses of the proletariat. Imperialism brings the working class to revolution.

. . . Imperialism is the export of capital to the sources of raw materials, the frantic struggle for exclusive monopoly of these sources, the struggle for redivision of the world that has already been divided, a struggle conducted with particular fury by new financial groups and powers seeking a "place in the sun" against the old ones which tightly cling to their prey. This frantic struggle between various groups of capitalists is remarkable in that an inevitable element of it is imperialist war, for the annexation of foreign territory. This fact in its turn is remarkable in that it leads to the weakening of the imperialists by one another, to the weakening of the position of capitalism in general; it accelerates the advent of the proletarian revolution and makes this revolution a practical necessity.

Ibid., p. 15, *Sotchinenia,* Vol. VI, pp. 72-73.

. . . imperialism has not only brought it about that revolution became a practical inevitability; it has also created favourable conditions for a direct attack on the citadels of capitalism.

Ibid., p. 16; *Sotchinenia,* Vol. VI, p. 74.

II. TACTICS

1) Maturity for Revolution

. . . concerning the prerequisites for the seizure of power by the proletariat. The opportunists assert that the proletariat cannot and ought not to seize power if it does not itself constitute a majority in the country. No proofs are adduced, for this absurd thesis cannot be justified either theoretically or practically. Let us admit this for a moment. Lenin replies to these gentlemen of the Second International. But suppose a historic situation arises (war, agrarian crisis, etc.) in which the proletariat, a minority of the population, is able to rally around itself the vast majority of the working masses, why should it not seize power then? Why should it not profit by the favourable internal and international situation to pierce the front of capitalism and hasten the general climax? . . . why not do it this way: first seize power, create favourable conditions for the development of the proletariat and then advance with seven-league strides to raise the cultural level of the working masses and form numerous cadres of leaders and administrators recruited from among the workers? Has not Russian experience demonstrated that these working class cadres of leaders are growing a hundred times more rapidly and thoroughly with the proletariat in power than under the rule of capital? Is it not obvious, that the experience of the revolutionary mass struggle ruthlessly refutes also this theoretical dogma of the opportunists?

Ibid., pp. 22 f.; *Sotchinenia,* Vol. VI, pp. 82-84.

Formerly, it was customary to talk of the existence or absence of objective conditions for the proletarian revolution in individual countries, or, to be more exact, in this or that advanced country. This point of view is now inadequate. Now we must say that objective conditions for the revolution exist throughout the whole system of imperialist world economy, which is an integral unit; the existence within this system of some countries that are not sufficiently developed from the industrial point of view cannot form an insurmountable obstacle to the revolution, *if* the system as a whole has become, or more correctly *because* the system as a whole has already become ripe for revolution.

Ibid., p. 32; *Sotchinenia,* Vol. VI, p. 96.

The Leninist theory of the revolution says: No, *not necessarily where industry is most developed,* and so forth; it will be broken where the chain of imperialism is weakest, for the proletarian revolution is the result of the breaking of the chain of the imperialist world front at its weakest link. The country which begins the revolution, which makes a breach in the capitalist front, may prove to be less developed in a capitalist sense than others which are more developed but have remained, nevertheless, within the framework of capitalism. . . . The chain proved to be weakest in Russia, although that country was less developed in a capitalistic sense than, for example, France, Germany, England or America.

Where in the near future will the chain be broken next? Once more, precisely where is it weakest. It is not impossible that this may be in India, for example. Why? Because there we find a young and militant revolutionary proletariat which has an ally in the shape of the national liberation movement, unquestionably a very powerful and important ally; because in that country the revolution faces a notorious enemy, a foreign imperialism, devoid of all moral authority and deservedly hated by the oppressed and exploited masses of India.

Ibid., pp. 33 f.; *Sotchinenia,* Vol. VI, pp. 97 f.

Marx and Engels said that at the end of the nineteenth century "the French will commence, and the Germans will finish"— the French will commence, because in the course of decades of revolution they acquired that fearless initiative in revolutionary action that made them the vanguard of the socialist revolution.

Today we see a different combination of the forces of international Socialism. We say that it is easier for the movement to start in those countries which are not exploiting countries, which have no opportunities for robbing easily, and are not able to bribe the upper stratum of their workers.

V. I. Lenin, "The Fundamental Tasks of the Party after the Seizure of Power by the Proletariat," *Selected Works,* Vol. VII, p. 281.

Things have turned out differently from what Marx and Engels expected. History has given us, the Russian toiling and exploited classes, the honourable role of vanguard of the international socialist revolution; and today we see clearly how far the development of the revolution will go.

Ibid., p. 282.

2) Maneuvering

The conclusion to be drawn is clear: To reject compromises "on principle," to reject the admissibility of compromises "on principle," to reject the admissibility of compromises in general, no matter of what kind, is childishness which is difficult to even take seriously. A statesman desirous of being useful to the revolutionary proletariat, must know how to single out concrete cases of precisely such compromises as are inadmissible, as express opportunism and treachery, and direct all the force of his criticism, the spearhead of merciless exposure and of relentless war, against those concrete compromises;

V. I. Lenin, "The Fundamental Principles of the Communist International and Its Second Congress," *Selected Works,* Vol. X, London, 1938, p. 76.

There are compromises and compromises. One must be able to analyse the situation and the concrete conditions of each compromise, or of each form of compromise. One must learn to distinguish between the man who gave the bandits the money and firearms in order to lessen the evil they had committed and to facilitate the task of capturing and shooting them, and the man who gives bandits money and firearms in order to share in the loot. In politics it is not always possible to do this so easily as in this childishly simple little example. But anyone who wanted to invent a recipe for the workers that would provide ready-made solutions for all cases that occur in life, or who promised that the politics of the revolutionary proletariat would never encounter difficult or intricate situations, would simply be a charlatan.

Ibid., pp. 76-77.

. . . encircle the proletariat on every side with a petty-bourgeois atmosphere, which permeates and corrupts the proletariat and causes constant relapses among the proletariat into petty-bourgeois spinelessness, disintegration, individualism, and alternate moods of exaltation and dejection. The strictest centralization and discipline are required in the political party of the proletariat in order to counteract this, in order that the organizational role of the proletariat (and this is its principal role) may be fulfilled correctly, successfully, victoriously.

Ibid., p. 84.

To carry on a war for the overthrow of the international bourgeoisie, a war which is a hundred times more difficult, prolonged and complicated than the most stubborn or ordinary wars between states, and to refuse beforehand to maneuver, to utilize the conflict of interests (even though temporary) among one's enemies, to refuse to temporise and compromise with possible (even though transient, unstable, vacillating and conditional) allies — is not this ridiculous in the extreme? Is it not as though in the difficult ascent of an unexplored and heretofore inaccessible mountain, we were to renounce beforehand the idea that at times we might have to go in zigzags, sometimes retracing our steps, sometimes abandoning the course once selected and trying various others?

Ibid., p. 111.

Some are of the opinion that Leninism is opposed to reforms, opposed to compromises and to agreements in general. That is absolutely untrue. Bolsheviks know as well as anybody else that in a certain sense "every little helps," that under certain conditions reforms, in general, and compromises and agreements, in particular, are necessary and useful.

J. Stalin, *Leninism I,* p. 84; *Sotchinenia,* Vol. VI, p. 165.

To a reformist, reforms are everything while revolutionary work is just something to talk about, a diversion. . . .

To a revolutionary, on the contrary, the main thing is revolutionary work and not reforms, to him reforms are by-products of the revolution. Therefore, with revolutionary tactics under the existing bourgeois regime reforms inevitably serve as instruments that disintegrate the regime, instruments that strengthen the revolution — a stronghold for the further development of the revolutionary movement.

The revolutionary will accept a reform in order to use it as a means wherewith to link legal work with illegal work, in order to use it as a screen behind which his illegal activities for the revolutionary preparation of the masses, for the overthrow of the bourgeoisie may be intensified.

> *Ibid.,* p. 85; *Sotchinenia,* Vol. VI, pp. 166 f.

The strictest loyalty to the ideas of Communism must be combined with the ability to make all the necessary practical compromises, to "tack," to make agreements, zigzags, retreats, and so on.
> Lenin, "Fundamental Principles of the Communist International," *Selected Works,* Vol. X, p. 138.

3) Use of Terror

Of course, we rejected individual terror only out of consideration of expediency; upon those who "on principle" were capable of condemning the terror of the Great French Revolution, or the terror in general employed by a victorious revolutionary party which is besieged by the bourgeoisie of the whole world — upon such people even Plekhanov in 1900-1903, when he was a Marxist and a revolutionary, heaped ridicule and scorn.

> V. I. Lenin, "Left-Wing Communism an Infantile Disorder," *Selected Works,* Vol. X, p. 72.

We have never rejected terror on principle, nor can we do so. Terror is a form of military operation that may be usefully applied, or may even be essential in certain moments of the battle, under certain conditions, and when the troops are in a certain condition. The point is, however, that terror is now advocated, not as one of the operations the army in the field must carry out in close connection and in complete harmony with the whole system of fighting, but as an individual attack, completely separated from any army whatever. In view of the absence of a central revolutionary organisation, terror cannot be anything but that.

V. I. Lenin, "Where to Begin?" *Selected Works,* Vol. II, London, 1936, p. 17.

May 17, 1921. Comrade Kursky, with reference to our conversation I enclose the draft of a complementary paragraph of the penal code. . . . * Its fundamental purpose is clear — to make plain to all the principle (politically true and no mere maxim of a narrow jurisprudence) which determines the character and justification of terrorism, its necessity and limits. The legal trial is not intended to replace terrorism; to make such a profession would be deception of others or oneself; but to base terrorism firmly on a fundamental principle and give it a legal form, unambiguous, without dishonesty or embellishment. The law must be couched in the widest possible terms, for only the revolutionary sense of justice and the revolutionary conscience will determine its more or less comprehensive application in practice.

> *Propaganda or agitation or participation in forming or co-operating with organisations designed to assist that portion of the industrial bourgeoisie which does not admit the right to existence of an economic system aiming at the destruction of capitalism, and which therefore attempts its forcible overthrow, whether by foreign intervention or blockade or espionage or financing the Press or by similar means, renders the delinquent subject to the supreme penalty. Under extenuating circumstances the capital penalty will be replaced by deprivation of liberty or by exile.

Lenin's letter published in *Bolshevik,* October 31, 1930, as quoted in W. Gurian, *Bolshevism: Theory and Practice,* London, Sheed & Ward, 1933, p. 302.

Question 7. Judicial powers of the G.P.U., trial without witnesses, without counsel, secret arrests. Considering that these measures are not approved of by French public opinion, it would be interesting to hear their justification. Is it intended to modify or abolish them?
Answer: The G.P.U. or the Cheka is a punitive organ of the Soviet government. It is more or less similar to the Committee of Public Safety which existed during the great French Revolution. It punishes primarily spies, plotters, terrorists, bandits, speculators and forgers. It is something in the nature of a military political tribunal set up for the purpose of protecting the interests of the revolution from attacks on the part of the counter-revolutionary bourgeoisie and their agents.

This organ was created on the day after the October Revolution, after all kinds of plots, terrorist and spying organisations financed by Russian and foreign capitalists were discovered. This organ developed and became consolidated after a series of terrorist acts had been perpetrated against the leaders of the soviet government. . . .
It must be admitted that the G.P.U. aimed at the enemies of the revolution without missing. By the way, this quality of the G.P.U. still holds good. It has been, ever since, the terror of the bourgeoisie, the indefatigable guard of the revolution, the unsheathed sword of the proletariat.

It is not surprising, therefore, that the bourgeoisie of all countries hate the G.P.U. All sorts of legends have been invented about the G.P.U.

The slander which has been circulated about the G.P.U. knows no bounds. And what does that mean? It means that the G.P.U. is properly defending the interests of the revolution. The sworn enemies of the revolution curse the G.P.U. Hence, it follows that the G.P.U. is doing the right thing.

But this is not how the workers regard the G.P.U. You go to the workers' districts and ask the workers what they think of it. You will find that they regard it with respect. Why? Because they see in it a loyal defender of the revolution.

I understand the hatred and distrust of the bourgeoisie for the G.P.U. I understand the various bourgeois tourists who, on coming to the U.S.S.R., inquire before anything else as to whether the G.P.U. still exists and whether the time has not yet come for its liquidation. This is comprehensible and not out of the ordinary. But I cannot understand some workers' delegates who, on coming to the U.S.S.R., ask with alarm as to whether many counter-revolutionaries have been punished by the G.P.U. and whether terrorists and plotters against the proletarian government will still be punished by it and is it not time yet for its dissolution. Why do some workers' delegates show such concern for the enemies of the proletarian revolution? How can it be explained? How can it be justified? They advocate a maximum of leniency, they advise the dissolution of the G.P.U. . . . But can anyone guarantee that the capitalists of all countries will abandon the idea of organising and financing counter-revolutionary plotters, terrorists, incendiaries and bomb-throwers after the liquidation of the G.P.U.? To disarm the revolution without having guarantees that the enemies of the revolution will be disarmed — would not that be folly, would not that be a crime against the working class? . . .

I do not mean to say by this that the internal situation of the country is such as makes it necessary to have punitive organs of the revolution. From the point of view of the internal situation, the revolution is so firm and unshakable that we could do without the G.P.U. But the trouble is that the enemies at home are not isolated individuals. They are connected in a thousand ways with the capitalists of all countries who support them by every means and in every way. We are a country surrounded by capitalist states. The internal enemies of our revolution are the agents of the capitalists of all countries. The capitalist states are the background and basis for the internal enemies of our revolution. In fighting against the enemies at home we fight the counter-revolutionary elements of all countries. Judge for yourselves whether under such conditions we can do without such punitive organs as the G.P.U.

No, comrades, we do not want to repeat the mistakes of the Paris Communards. The G.P.U. is necessary for the revolution and it will continue to live and strike terror into the hearts of the enemies of the proletariat. [Loud applause.]

Stalin, "Interview with Foreign Workers' Delegations. Answer

127

to the French Delegation, November 5, 1927," *Leninism I,* pp. 419 f.

III. The Party

If we begin with the solid foundation of a strong organisation of revolutionaries, we can guarantee the stability of the movement as a whole and carry out the aims of both Social-Democracy, and of trade unionism. If, however, we begin with a wide workers' organisation, supposed to be most "accessible" to the masses, when as a matter of fact it will be most accessible to the gendarmes and will make the revolutionaries most accessible to the police, we shall achieve the aims neither of Social-Democracy nor of trade unionism; we shall not escape from our primitiveness. . . .

V. I. Lenin, "What is to be Done," *Selected Works,* Vol. II, p. 134.

Point 1 of the rules defined what was meant by the term, member of the Party. The definition I proposed in my draft was as follows: "A member of the R.S.D.L.P. is one who recognizes its programme and supports the Party materially as well as by personal participation in one of the organisations of the Party." Martov, on the other hand, moved to substitute for the words underlined the words: working under the control and guidance of one of the organisations of the Party. We insisted that membership of the Party must be given a narrow definition so as to distinguish those who worked from those who talked, so as to get rid of chaos in the matter of organisation, to get rid of the monstrosity and absurdity of having organisations which consisted of members of the Party, but which were not Party organisations, etc. Martov was in favour of widening the Party and spoke of a broad class movement which demanded a broad — a diffuse — organisation, etc.

Ibid., "The Second Congress and the Split in the R.S.D.L.P.," pp. 349-350.

. . . I am not at all frightened by terrible words about "a state of siege in the Party," about "exceptional laws against individual persons and groups," and so forth. In regard to unstable and wavering elements, it is not only our right but our duty to create "a state of siege," and the whole of our Party rules, of our centralism now ratified by the Congress, is nothing but "a state of siege" against numerous sources of political diffusiveness. It is precisely against diffusiveness that we need special, even exceptional laws, and the step taken by the Congress has indicated the right political direction, by creating a reliable basis for such laws and such measures. (Speech delivered September 2 (August 20), 1903).

Ibid., pp. 364-365.

As a matter of fact, the entire position of the opportunists in questions of organisation began to be revealed in the course of the controversy over point 1: their advocacy of a diffuse and loose Party organisation; their hostility to the idea (the "bureaucratic" idea) of building the Party from above, starting from the Party Congress and the bodies emanating from the latter; their tendency to proceed from below, a tendency which would allow every professor, every schoolboy, and "every striker" to register himself as a member of the Party; their hostility to the "formalism" which demands that a Party member belong to an organisation recognised by the Party; their inclination towards the mentality of the bourgeois intellectual who is only prepared "platonically to recognise organisational relations"; their weakness for opportunist profundity and for anarchist phrases; their partiality for autonomism as against centralism. . . .

Ibid., "One Step Forward, Two Steps Back," pp. 408-409.

Only after the proletarian dictatorship will have deprived the bourgeoisie of such powerful weapons of effective influence as the press, the school, the parliament, the church, the administrative apparatus, etc., only after the final defeat of the bourgeois social order will have become evident for everyone, only then will all or practically all the workmen begin to enter the ranks of the Communist Party.

"Resolutions on the Role of the Communist Party in the Proletarian Revolution—Second Congress of the Communist International, 1920. *Pravda,* July 30, 1920.

Each change in the life of our Party, in the life of our socialist state and its army, has required a concrete reorganization of party

129

ranks and this brought changes in Party resolutions and the charter of the CPSU(b). But despite all the changes in organisational forms and methods of work, our Party has always remained true to its organisational principles. These organisational principles were worked out in the laying of its foundations. In the charter of the CPSU(b) adopted at the 18th Congress of the Party, the basic principles of Party organisation in the Soviet Army were set forth.

"Talks on Charter of CPSU(b)," *Krasnaya Zvezda* (Red Star), October 22, 1946.

Up to the present day our Party has resembled a hospitable, patriarchal family, which is ready to accept all sympathizers. But since the time that our Party became a centralized organization, it has thrown off its patriarchal countenance and has become completely like a citadel, whose doors open only to the worthy.

J. Stalin, "Class of the Proletariat and Party of the Proletariat" (1905), *Sotchinenia*, Vol. I, Moscow, 1946, p. 67.

In the Party, the decisions of the congress are obligatory also upon those who doubt the correctness of a decision. . . . Our Party is strong through the fact that the decisions of the majority are obligatory upon all not only in form, but in substance.

M. Kalinin, "Speech to XIVth Congress of Russian Communist Party" (1925), *Stenographic Report of 14th Party Congress,* Moscow, 1926, p. 321.

In order to effect strict discipline within the Party and in all Soviet work and to secure the greatest unity in removing all factionalism, the congress authorises the C.C. (Central Committee) to apply all Party penalties, including expulsion, in cases of breach of discipline or of reviving or engaging in factionalism; and in regard to members of the Central Committee to reduce them to the status of candidates and, as an extreme measure, to expel them from the Party. A necessary condition for the application of such an extreme measure to members of the C.C., candidates of the C.C. and members of the Control Commission is the convocation of the plenum of the C.C., to which all candidates of the C.C. and all members of the Control Commission shall be invited. If such an assembly of the most responsible leaders of the Party, by a two-thirds majority, deems it necessary to reduce a member of the C.C. to the status of candidate, or to expel him from the Party, this measure must be put into effect immediately. (March 1921)

> V. I. Lenin, "Preliminary Draft of the Resolution of the Tenth Congress of the R.C.P.(B), on Party Unity," *Selected Works,* Vol. IX, London, 1937, p. 134.

He (Lutovinov) wants real democracy, that all, at least the most important questions should be discussed in all the cells from bottom up, that the whole Party should get going on every question and should take part in the consideration of that question. But, comrades, with such an arrangement our party would be transformed into a discussion club of eternally jabbering and never-deciding people, while our party must, above all, be an acting one, because we are in power. Besides . . . there is no reason to suppose that the enemies who surround us are not engaged in some preparatory work for blockade or intervention. That is the situation. Can we in such circumstances carry all questions of war and peace into the street? Yet, to discuss a question in 20,000 cells means to carry the question out into the street. . . . It must be remembered, that in the conditions of being surrounded by enemies, a sudden stroke on our part, an unexpected maneuver, speed, decide everything. What would have become of us, if, instead of discussing our political campaign for the Lausanne Conference in an intimate circle of trusted persons of the Party, we had carried all that work out into the street, revealed our cards? Enemies would have discounted all the minuses and pluses, undermined our campaign, and we should have departed from Lausanne in shame. What would become of us if we should first bring out into the street the question of war and peace — the most important of all important questions. . . . Why, we should be given a sound thrashing to the count of two. It is clear, comrades, that for organizational as well as political reasons Comrade Lutovinov's democracy is a utopia. It is unfair and unnecessary.

> J. Stalin's "Report to the XIIth Congress of the Russian Communist Party(b), April 17-25, 1923," Moscow 1923, pp. 181-182.

The history of the Party teaches us, first of all, that the victory of the proletarian revolution, the victory of the dictatorship of the proletariat, is impossible without a revolutionary party of the proletariat, a party free from the opportunism, irreconcilable towards compromisers and capitulators, and revolutionary in its attitude towards the bourgeoisie and its state power. The history of the Party teaches us that to leave the proletariat without such a party means to leave it without revolutionary leadership, and to leave it without revolutionary leadership means to ruin the cause of the proletarian revolution.

The history of the Party teaches us that the ordinary Social-Democratic Party of the West-European type, brought up under conditions of civil peace, trailing in the wake of the opportunists, dreaming of "social reforms," and dreading social revolution, cannot be such a party.

> *History of the Communist Party of the Soviet Union,* New York, 1939, p. 353.

The history of the Party further teaches us that a party of the working class cannot perform the role of leader of its class, cannot perform the role of organizer and leader of the proletarian revolution, unless it has mastered the advanced theory of the working-class movement, the Marxist-Leninist theory.

The power of the Marxist-Leninist theory lies in the fact that it enables the Party to find the right orientation in any situation, to understand the inner connection of current events, to foresee their course and to perceive not only how and in what direction they are developing in the present, but how and in what direction they are bound to develop in the future.

> *Ibid.,* p. 355.

Mastering the Marxist-Leninist theory means being able to enrich this theory with the new experience of the revolutionary movement, with new propositions and conclusions, it means being able to *develop it and advance it* without hesitating to replace — in accordance with the substance of the theory — such of its propositions and conclusions as have become antiquated by new ones corresponding to the new historical situation.

Ibid., p. 356.

The history of the Party further teaches us that unless the Party of the working class wages an uncompromising struggle against the opportunists within its own ranks, unless it smashes the capitulators in its own midst, it cannot preserve unity and discipline within its ranks, it cannot perform its role of organizer and leader of the proletarian revolution, nor its role as the builder of the new, Socialist society.

Ibid., p. 359.

IV. Relations With the Non-Communist World

We are living not merely in a state but in a system of states and the existence of the Soviet Republic side by side with imperialist states for a long time is unthinkable. One or the other must triumph in the end. And before that end supervenes, a series of frightful collisions between the Soviet Republic and the bourgeois states will be inevitable. That means that if the ruling class, the proletariat, wants to hold sway, it must prove its capacity to do so by its military organization also. . . .

V. I. Lenin, "Report of Central Committee at 8th Party Congress" of March 18, 1919, *Selected Works*, Vol. VIII, p. 33.

Those who were in favour of peace and who inculcated into the minds of the lovers of ostentation that one must be able to calculate the relation of forces and not help the imperialists by making the war against socialism easier for them, while socialism is still weak, and when the chances of the war are manifestly against socialism, were right, and have been proved right by the course of events.

V. I. Lenin, " 'Left-Wing' Childishness and Petty-Bourgeois Mentality," *Selected Works*, Vol. VII, p. 353.

Most probably, the world revolution will develop along the line of a series of new countries dropping out of the system of the imperialist countries as a result of revolution, while the proletarians of these countries will be supported by the proletariat of the imperialist

133

states. We see that the first country to win is already supported by the workers and toiling masses of other countries. Without this support it could not maintain itself. Beyond a doubt, this support will grow and become stronger. But it is likewise beyond a doubt that the very process of the breaking away of a number of new countries from imperialism will be more rapid and more thorough, the more thoroughly socialism fortifies itself in the first victorious country the faster this country is transformed into the basis for the further unfolding of the world revolution, into the lever for the further disintegration of imperialism.

> Stalin, *Leninism, I,* p. 135; *Sotchinenia,* Vol. VI, pp. 398-399.

We cannot forget the saying of Lenin to the effect that a great deal in the matter of our construction depends on whether we succeed in delaying war with the capitalist countries, which is inevitable but which may be delayed either until proletarian revolution ripens in Europe or until colonial revolutions come to a head, or, finally, until the capitalists fight among themselves over the division of the colonies. Therefore, the maintenance of peaceful relations with capitalist countries is an obligatory task for us. The basis of our relations with capitalist countries consists in admitting the co-existence of two opposed systems.

> J. Stalin, "Speech to the 15th Congress of the Soviet Union, December 2, 1927," *Sotchinenia,* Vol. X, Moscow, 1949, p. 288.

An extraordinarily difficult and dangerous situation in international affairs; the necessity of maneuvering and retreating; a period of waiting for new outbreaks of the revolution which is maturing in the West at a painfully slow pace; within the country a period of slow construction and ruthless "tightening up," of prolonged and persistent struggle waged by stern, proletarian discipline against the menacing element of petty-burgeois laxity and anarchy—such in brief are the distinguishing features of the special stage of the socialist revolution we are now living in.

> V. I. Lenin, "The Immediate Tasks of the Soviet Government," *Selected Works,* Vol. VII, pp. 348-349.

The fact that the Soviet Union and the greatly shaken capitalist countries showed themselves to be in one powerful camp, ranged against the fascist aggressors, showed that the struggle of two systems within the democratic camp was temporarily alleviated, suspended, but this of course does not mean the end of this struggle.

E. Varga, in *World Economy and World Politics,* Moscow, June 1949, p. 11.

. . . until the international socialist revolution breaks out, embraces several countries and is strong enough to overcome international imperialism, it is the bounden duty of the Socialists, who have conquered in one country (especially a backward one), not to accept battle against the giants of imperialism. Their duty is to try to avoid war, to wait until the conflicts between the imperialists weaken them still more, and bring the revolution in other countries still nearer.

V. I. Lenin, " 'Left-Wing' Childishness and Petty Bourgeois Mentality," *Selected Works,* Vol. VII, p. 353.

Socialism is inconceivable without large-scale capitalist technique based on the last word of modern science; it is inconceivable without planned state organisation which subjects tens of millions of people to the strictest observance of a single standard in production and distribution.

Ibid., p. 365.

To recognize defence of one's fatherland means recognising the legitimacy and justice of war. Legitimacy and justice from what point of view? Only from the point of view of the socialist proletariat and its struggle for emancipation. We do not recognise any other point of view. If war is waged by the exploiting class with the object of strengthening its class rule, such a war is a criminal war, and "defencism" in such a war is a base betrayal of socialism. If war is waged by the proletariat after it has conquered the bourgeoisie in its own country, and is waged with the object of strengthening and extending socialism, such a war is legitimate and "holy." We have been "defencists" since November 7 (October 25) 1917.

Ibid., p. 357.

The tasks of the Party in foreign policy are: 1) to utilize each and every contradiction and conflict among the surrounding capitalist groups and governments for the purpose of disintegrating imperialism; 2) to spare no pains or means to render assistance to the proletarian revolutions in the West; 3) to take all necessary measures to strengthen the national liberation movement in the East; 4) to strengthen the Red Army.

> J. Stalin, "Party After Seizure of Power," *Pravda*, August 28, 1921. Cf. *Sotchinenia*, Vol. V, Moscow, 1947, p. 111.

Since the time the Soviet republics were formed, the states of the world have split into two camps; the camp of socialism and the camp of capitalism. In the camp of capitalism we have imperialists, war, national enmity, oppression, colonial slavery, and supernationalism. In the camp of the Soviets, the camp of socialism, on the contrary, we have mutual confidence, national equality, and the peaceful co-existence and fraternal collaboration of people.

> J. Stalin, *Pravda*, December 28, 1922. Cf. *Sotchinenia*, Vol. V, p. 154.

In the period of the October Revolution Lenin taught the Party how to advance fearlessly and resolutely when conditions favored an advance. In the period of the Brest-Litovsk peace Lenin taught the Party how to retreat in good order when the forces of the enemy are obviously superior to our own, in order to prepare with the utmost energy for a new offensive.

> *Short History of the CPSU(b)*, Foreign Languages Publishing House, Moscow, 1945, p. 219.

. . . Unlike Hitlerite Germany, the Soviet Union and its allies are waging a war for liberation — a just war for the liberation of the enslaved peoples of Europe and the U.S.S.R. from Hitler's tyranny. Therefore, all honest people must support the armies of the U.S.S.R., Great Britain and the other allies as armies of liberation. We have not nor can we have such war aims as the seizure of foreign territories or the conquest of other peoples, irrespective of whether European peoples and territories, or Asiatic people and territories, including Iran, are concerned. Our first aim is to liberate our territories and our peoples from the German Nazi yoke.

We have not nor can we have such war aims as the imposition of our will and our regime on the Slavic and other enslaved peoples of Europe who are waiting for our help. Our aim is to help these peoples in their struggle for liberation from Hitler's tyranny, and then to accord them the possibility of arranging their lives on their own land as they think fit, with absolute freedom. No interference of any kind with the domestic affairs of other nations!

> J. Stalin, as Chairman of the State Defence Committee: Speech to the Moscow Soviet on the Anniversary of the October Revolution, Moscow, November 6, 1941. *Pravda,* November 7, 1941, quoted in *War and Peace Aims of the United Nations,* Louise W. Holborn, ed., World Peace Foundation, Boston, 1943.

But the Soviet Union, building Communism in conditions of capitalist encirclement, is not guaranteed against the danger of attack from the outside and against attempts to restore capitalism. . . . The war (of 1941-45) ended with the complete defeat of Hitler Germany. But so long as the capitalist world exists, the possibility of a new war and of bandit attacks on the U.S.S.R. are not excluded.

Krasny Flot (Red Fleet), July 18, 1946.

At present the only determining criterion of revolutionary proletarian internationalism is: are you for or against the U.S.S.R., the Motherland of the world proletariat? An internationalist is not one who verbally recognizes international solidarity or sympathizes with it. A real internationalist is one who brings his sympathy and recognition up to the point of practical and maximal help to the U.S.S.R. in support and defense of the U.S.S.R. by every means and in every possible form. Actual cooperation with the U.S.S.R., the readiness of the workers of any country to subject all their aims to the basic problem of strengthening the U.S.S.R. in their struggle — this is the manifestation of revolutionary proletarian internationalism on the part of workmen in foreign countries. . . . The defense of the U.S.S.R., as of the socialist motherland of the world proletariat, is the holy duty of every honest man everywhere and not only of the citizens of the U.S.S.R.

> A. J. Vyshinsky, "Communism and the Motherland," *Voprosy Filosofii* (Problems of Philosophy), No. 2, 1948.

While expanding peaceful socialist construction, we must not forget for a minute the intrigues of the international reaction, which is hatching the plans of a new war. It is necessary to bear in mind the instructions of the great Lenin that, having passed to peaceful labor, it is necessary to continue being on the alert, and guard like the apple of one's eye the armed forces and the defense potential of our country.

> Stalin, Order No. 7, May 1, 1946, as Minister of Armed Forces, *Izvestia* and *Pravda,* May 1, 1946.

Soviet diplomacy in its general purpose as well as in its methods differs categorically from the diplomacy of the feudal epoch and the epoch of the bourgeois domination. The principle aim of the Soviet Diplomacy was and will be concentrated on the study of factors of social importance. For this purpose, Soviet Diplomacy has at its disposal unsurpassed Marxist-Leninist methods of perception of World conditions and to a certain degree also of conditions — in the full meaning of that word — connected with the economical, political, historical, class and other problems of the country with which it deals. It is necessary to always remember J. V. Stalin's words: " . . . in order to avoid mistakes in politics and not to fall into the circle of idle dreamers, the Party of the Proletariat must proceed in its activity not from the abstract "principles of human intelligence" but from the concrete conditions of material life of society as the decisive power of the social developments." Marxist-Leninist theory "gives the Party the possibility of orienting itself in the situation, to understand the internal connections of the surrounding occurrences, to foresee the course of events and to recognize not only that how and where the events will develop at the present time but also how and where they should develop in the future." Here in this foresight and recognition of the present and future events, and not in the deceit and intrigues consists the strength of the Soviet Diplomacy, which so brilliantly justified itself during the whole history of its activity. For its honest aim — the security of peace within its own borders as well as in the whole world on the basis of friendship with its neighbors, the close and remote — honest methods are sufficient.

> A. J. Vyshinsky and S. A. Lozovsky, editors, *Diplomaticheskij Slovar,* Vol. I, Moscow, 1948, "Diplomacy," pp. 591-592.

DOCUMENTS AND SOURCE MATERIAL

V. CULTURAL AND EDUCATIONAL POLICIES

a) General Aim

We took over the old state apparatus, and this was unfortunate for us. Very often the state apparatus works against us. In 1917, after we captured power, the situation was that the apparatus sabotaged us. This frightened us very much and we pleaded with the state officials: "Please come back." They all came back, but this was unfortunate for us. We now have a vast number of state employees, but we lack sufficiently educated forces who could really control them. Actually, it often happens that at the top, as it were, where we have state power, the apparatus functions somehow; but down below, where these state officials function, they function in such a way that very often they counteract our measures. At the top, we have, I don't know how many, but at all events, I think, several thousand, at the utmost several tens of thousands, of our own people. Down below, however, there are hundreds of thousands of old officials who came over to us from the tsar and from bourgeois society and who, sometimes unconsciously, work against us. Certainly nothing can be done here in a short period of time. Here we must work many years in order to improve the apparatus, to change it and to enlist new forces. We are doing this fairly quickly, perhaps too quickly. Soviet schools and Workers' Faculties have been formed, several hundreds of thousands of young people are studying, studying too fast perhaps, but at all events, the work has been started, and I think it will bear fruit. If we do not work too hurriedly we shall within a few years have a large number of young people who will be capable of radically changing our apparatus.

V. I. Lenin, "Five Years of the Russian Revolution and the Prospects of the World Revolution," *Selected Works*, Vol X, pp. 330-331.

Introduce accurate and conscientious accounting of money, manage economically, do not be lazy, do not steal, observe the strictest discipline during work — it is precisely such slogans, which were justly scorned by the revolutionary proletariat when the bour-

geoisie concealed its rule as an exploiting class by these command-
ments, that now, after the overthrow of the bourgeoisie, are becoming the immediate and the principal slogans of the moment.

> V. I. Lenin, "The Immediate Tasks of the Soviet Govern-
> ment," *Selected Works,* Vol. VII, pp. 317-318.

As a result of the immense cultural work in U.S.S.R., a numerous
new Soviet intelligentsia has arisen in our country, an intelligentsia
which has emerged from the ranks of the working class, peasantry
and Soviet employees, which is of the flesh and blood of our people,
which has never known the yoke of exploitation, which hates exploiters, and which is ready to serve the peoples of the U.S.S.R.
faithfully and devotedly. I think that the rise of this new socialist
intelligentsia of the people is one of the most important results of
the current revolution in our country.

> J. Stalin, "Report on work of the Central Committee to 18th
> Congress of CPSU(b)," (March 10, 1939). *Stenograficheskii
> otchet,* Moscow, 1939, p. 25.

The embezzlers of public property who, for the sake of their personal gain, cause damage to the socialist state have not yet died out.
The fight with those violators of state laws must be grim and
merciless. In that fight it is extremely important that the Soviet
people maintain perpetual vigilance against all kinds of violators
of the rules of the socialist community who, for the sake of personal gain, resort to embezzlement, bribes, and graft and who hurt
the honest workers of our country by their criminal conduct. The
fight with petty-bourgeois laxity in production and institutions, an
honorable attitude toward work, and a careful attitude toward
public socialist property are the prime requirements of Communist morality.

> Editorial "Communist Morality," *Bolshevik,* No. 15, August
> 1946, p. 23.

Capitalist encirclement must not be forgotten for a moment. It
would be incorrect and naive to think that Communist morality
has been completely affirmed and has triumphed in our country. It

must not be forgotten that Soviet people came from the bowels of capitalist society. The "birthmarks" of capitalist consciousness have remained with many of them. . . .

"Morals of Soviet Man," *Trud*, May 24, 1947, p. 1.

The Soviet social and political regime comprises no elements which bring out any vicious tendencies. Thieves and rogues are remnants of the distant past, still existing as a result of the capitalist environment and its ideology which is alien to the socialist manner of life.

Golyakov, in *Sovietskoye Gosudarstvo i Pravo* (Soviet State and Law), No. 7, 1947.

Without further raising the social consciousness and without vigorous efforts to overcome the survivals of capitalism in the minds of the people, it is impossible to carry out with success the tasks of Communist construction in the country. . . . Lenin-Stalin ideology must instill a hatred for the capitalist order, and the lying, hypocritical bourgeois ideology, whose purport is to deceive the masses. . . . We should not for a minute forget that the field of culture and ideology is a field of violent and stubborn struggle. By its very character, socialist ideology and the culture of the Soviet people is opposed to bourgeois culture and must wage a struggle against it.

"Lenin and Stalin on Party Ideology," *Partiinaya Zhizn,* (Party Life), No. 1, 1947, pp. 11, 19, 20.

If for some reason our party propaganda goes lame, if the Marxist-Leninist training of our cadres begins to languish, if our work of raising the political and theoretical level of the cadres lags and the cadres themselves cease on account of this to show interest in the prospect becoming narrow plodders with no outlook, blindly and mechanically carrying out instructions from above — then our entire state and Party work must inevitably languish.

J. Stalin, "Report on Work of Central Committee to CPSU(b) at 18th Congress," (March 10, 1939). *Stenograficheskii otchet,* Moscow 1939, p. 30.

The Soviet school cannot be satisfied to rear merely educated persons. Basing itself on the facts and deductions of progressive science,

141

it should instill the ideology of Communism in the minds of the young generation, shape a Marxist-Leninist world outlook and inculcate the spirit of Soviet patriotism and Bolshevik ideas in them.

"For Further Progress in Soviet Schools," *Kultura i Zhizn* (Culture and Life), August 31, 1947.

b)   The Control of Cultural Life

One of the fundamental questions of socialist realism is the question of art's spirit. Our Soviet Society develops under the banner of the only correct scientific theory of social development under the banner of Marx's, Engel's, Lenin's and Stalin's teachings. At present, when in our country all exploitation classes are liquidated, the very ground on which the exploitation of man by man would grow, is destroyed, when socialism is built up, the further movement of the Soviet people toward Communism depends upon a successful organization of spiritual-educational work among the toiling masses.

The role of the socialist consciousness as the factor of social development grew immeasurably. From the grade of this consciousness depends in a large degree the further victories of the Soviet people. . . . Marxist-Leninist esthetics always fought against those reactionary theories which attempted to prove that literature and art do not have any practical significance in social life but only raise esthetical emotions in persons and only serve as a tool for amusement and pleasure. . . . The adherents of the theory "art for art" do not promote the art but humiliate it, excluding the social motives and transforming it into empty amusement of the sluggards. . . .

In Marxist-Leninist esthetics art and literature are regarded as mighty instruments for the education of the people, instruments for the ideological struggle against the barbarous, decadent culture of modern capitalism. This is why the Party Central Committee decisions on ideological matters stressed the ideological-political significance of the arts and literature with such emphasis. Our magazines, the August 14, 1946, decree of the Party Central Committee points out, cannot be indifferent to politics. . . .

The Party has resolutely condemned those magazine editors and heads of literary organizations who thought that politics is a matter for the government, a matter for the Party Central Committee, and that the duty of the writer is merely to write a work well and

142

artistically without thinking about politics. The writer's duty is to be guided in all his work by that without which the Soviet system cannot live, i.e., its policy of educating youth in the spirit of the high ideals of communism. It is necessary to fight resolutely against all attempts to revise this most important tenet of Marxism-Leninism. . . .

Soviet writers and workers in other forms of art view rootless cosmopolitans with scorn and fight irreconcilably against them. Cosmopolitan antipatriots have monstrously distorted the Leninist-Stalinist conception of internationalism. They have adopted a scornful attitude to national cultures, above all to the great Russian culture.

> "Soviet Literature on the Upgrade," *Bolshevik,* No. 14, July 1951, pp. 1-10.

Every literary work which contains a talented exposition of the theme of love for one's socialist motherland inspires in our hearts great patriotic feelings.

Unfortunately, Sosyura's poem "Love the Ukraine" does not engender such feelings. What is more, it evokes a feeling of disillusionment and protest. It is true, in his poem the poet calls for love of the Ukraine. The question arises: *Which* Ukraine is in question, of *which* Ukraine is Sosyura singing? . . .

Out of time, out of historical epoch — this is the Ukraine in the poet's portrayal.

Sosyura's poem does not contain the image which is infinitely dear to every true patriot — the image of our socialist motherland, of the Soviet Ukraine.

> "Against Ideological Distortions in Literature," *Pravda,* July 2, 1951, p. 2. Cf. *The Current Digest of the Soviet Press,* Vol. III, No. 24, p. 13.

Letter to the Editors of *Pravda* (By V. Sosyura).
Dear Comrades: I earnestly request you to print the following in your newspaper. *Pravda,* July 2, 1951, carried an article "Against Ideological Distortions in Literature" sharply and justly criticizing my poem "Love the Ukraine."

143

I consider this criticism to be absolutely correct; I have grasped profoundly the fact that the Soviet Ukraine cannot be conceived in separation from the mighty growth of our multinational state. The Ukraine, after all, won its happiness with the fraternal assistance of the great Russian people and the other peoples of our motherland. Only thanks to the leadership of our Party and of the deeply beloved leader of our peoples, Comrade Stalin, has the Ukraine become what it is. . . .

The criticism of me in *Pravda* is a bitter but merited lesson, a lesson which will give me strength to so sharpen the weapon of my poetry, in which matter our Party will help me, that never again in any way will I make such inadmissible errors in my creative work, that it will always and everywhere serve only our socialist people, that the nationalists, who never loved and do not love our people, who can never be called Ukrainians and who have nothing in common with our people, as darkness has nothing in common with the sun, may not make use of a single line of my verse.

Dear Comrades! I am very grateful to you for your correct, Bolshevist criticism, aimed at the ruthless uprooting of survivals of the past in the minds of people, aimed at rectifying and not destroying, at bettering and not worsening. . . .

Pravda, July 10, 1951, p. 4. Cf. *The Current Digest of the Soviet Press,* Vol. III, No. 25, p. 9.

In well-known decrees on ideological questions, the Party Central Committee has called on writers and artists to educate Soviet youth to be ideological, optimistic, joyous, ready to overcome any difficulties on the path of construction of communism. The above verses by Simonov and still more those published in the large single volume "Verses, Plays and Stories," not included among the selected verses but distributed in many thousands of copies, do not meet the requirements of the Party. Furthermore, these verses lead youth away from communal interests to individualism. . . .

The verse contains not the slightest echo of the ideas of our time. Before us is the outline of a melancholy-minded gentleman with a glass in his hand. If "1947" had not been written under the verse, we might have dated it 1847 or any other year of the past century.

In another verse the outline of the same melancholy gentleman rises before the reader, no longer with the glass, but with an after-dinner pipe. In a third a lamb is eulogized. . . .

Naturally, Soviet people not only know how to work with inspiration for the good of society, but they also know how to relax and enjoy themselves and love. But all this is nothing like what Simonov portrays in certain of his verses. The life of the Soviet people is permeated with lofty communal interests. But many of Simonov's verses only portray eroticism. "He" and "she"— there is nothing, nothing else in the world and no other interests.

> "What is Living and What is Dead in K. Simonov's Poetry," *Komsomolskaya Pravda*, July 10, 1951, p. 3. Cf. *The Current Digest of the Soviet Press*, Vol. III, No. 26, p. 5.

The *Pravda* editorial article (see *Pravda*, July 20, 1951, pp. 2-3) criticized strongly the weak libretto of the opera "Bogdan Khmelnitsky," the authors of which are W. Wasilewska and A. Korneichuk. Wasilewska and I completely accept this just criticism. What were our mistakes? Above all, we deviated from the historical truth, our libretto did not show the struggle of the Ukrainian people with the Polish nobility which for centuries oppressed the Ukrainian people. We did not show, also, the terrible condition of the Ukrainian people beneath the yoke of the Polish nobility, we did not deal convincingly with the theme of the war of liberation of the Ukrainian people. These mistakes could not fail to be reflected in the characterization of many of the main heroes of "Bogdan Khmelnitsky." Our idea that, if showed the defeat of the Polish nobility, we might in so doing in some degree offend the national dignity of the Polish people, this idea was wrong. It was wrong because the Polish nobility was the enemy not only of the Ukrainian but also of the Polish people.

Pravda's editorial article on the opera "Bogdan Khmelnitsky" ends with the words: "The Soviet audience awaits a good Soviet opera on (this) important historical subject." Allow me to assure you that W. Wasilewska and the composer, K. Dankevich, will do all we can to justify the hopes of our Soviet audience. . . .

The Bolshevist party and the great Stalin personally, the best friend of the Ukrainian people, have helped the people of the Soviet Ukraine to defeat and extirpate the venomous nationalist growth. Under the direction of and with the help of the Central Committee of the C.P.S.U. and the Central Committee of the Communist Party of the Ukraine, Ukrainian Soviet writers have dealt a crushing blow to the agents of the enemy in our literature.

A. Korneichuk's report on "Ideological Distortions in Literature Exposed by the *Pravda's* Article and Current Tasks of Writers of the Soviet Ukraine."

> Plenary Session of the Board of the Union of Soviet Writers of the Ukraine, *Literaturnaya Gazeta*, August 2, 1951, pp. 2-3. Cf. *The Current Digest of the Soviet Press*, Vol. III, No. 29, p. 21.

The fact that the book (The History of Philosophy by Alexandrov) did not produce any important protest, that an intervention of the Central Committee and of Comrade Stalin himself was required in order to uncover the shortcomings of the work, proves that there is no Bolshevik criticism and self-criticism on the philosophic front. The well-known decisions of the Central Committee were directed against lack of ideas and non-political attitudes in literature, against separation from topics of our time; against subservience to foreigners for a fighting Bolshevik Party attitude in literature and art.

> A. A. Zhdanov, Speech in the Discussion on G. F. Alexandrov's book, *Bolshevik*, August 30, 1947, pp. 18, 20.

Three years ago the Central Committee of our party accepted a resolution on the opera: The great friendship of W. Muradeli. The Central Committee has severely condemned the anti-popular, formalistic directives in art; it has clearly formulated the tasks of Soviet music which are determined by the high principles of Soviet realism.

Our Party, Comrade Stalin, have shown great care about the development of Soviet music, they have called upon all Soviet composers to use the way of socialist realism . . . to create such musical works which would help the Soviet people in its fight for the building of Communism.

> T. Chrennikov, "The New Upswing of Soviet Music," *Bolshevik*, No. 3, February, 1951, p. 27.

146

c) The Fight Against Religion

Religion is not a private affair in relation to the Party of the Socialist proletariat. Our Party is a league of class-conscious and advanced fighters for the emancipation of the working class. Such a league must not be indifferent to unenlightenment, ignorance and obscurantism in the form of religious beliefs. We demand the complete separation of the church from the state in order to combat religious darkness with a purely ideological, and exclusively ideological, weapon, our printed and oral propaganda. One reason why we have founded our [Party] is just to wage such a fight against all religious stultification of the workers. For us therefore the ideological fight is not a private affair but a general affair of the Party and the proletariat.

> Lenin, "Socialism and Religion," *Selected Works*, Vol. II, p. 660.

But a slave who has realised his slavery and has risen up to fight for his emancipation is already only half a slave. The present-day class-conscious worker, trained by large-scale factory industry and educated by urban life, rejects religious superstitions with contempt, leaves heaven to the priests and the bourgeois hypocrites and fights for a better life here on earth. The modern proletariat is coming over to Socialism, which enlists science in the struggle against religious obscurity and emancipates the workers from belief in a life hereafter by welding them together for a real fight for a better life on earth.

Religion should be declared a private affair — these are the words in which the attitude of Socialists to religion is customarily expressed. But the meaning of these words must be precisely defined so as to leave no room for misunderstanding. We demand that religion should be a private affair as far as the state is concerned, but under no circumstances can we regard religion as a private affair as far as our own party is concerned. The state must not be concerned with religion, religious societies should have no connection with the state power. Everybody must be absolutely free to profess any religion he pleases or not to believe in any religion at all, that is, to be an atheist, as every Socialist usually is. No distinction whatever between citizens, as regards their rights, depending upon their religious beliefs can be tolerated. Every reference to the belief of citizens must be unconditionally expunged from all official documents. There must be absolutely no subsidies to a state church, no grants of government funds to church and religious societies, which must become associations absolutely free and independent of the state, associations of citizens holding the same ideas. Only the complete fulfillment of these demands can put an end to the disgraceful and accursed past, when the church was in feudal dependence on the state and the Russian citizens were in feudal dependence on the state church, when medieval, inquisitorial laws existed and were enforced (laws which to this day remain on our criminal statute books), laws which prosecuted people for their faith or lack of faith, which did violence to the conscience of man, which associated government posts and government incomes with the distribution of the state-clerical gin. The complete separation of the church from the state — that is the demand which the Socialist proletariat makes of the modern state and the modern church....

> Lenin, "Socialism and Religion," *Selected Works*, Vol. XI, pp. 658-59.

... a magazine that sets out to be an organ of militant materialism must be a fighting organ in the first place, ... must be an organ of militant atheism. We have departments, or at least state institutions, which are in charge of this work. But this work is being carried on extremely apathetically and extremely unsatisfactorily, and is apparently suffering from the general conditions of our truly Russian (even though Soviet) bureaucracy. It is therefore highly essential that in addition to the work of these state institutions, and in order to improve and infuse life into this work, a magazine which sets out to be an organ of militant materialism should carry on untiring atheist propaganda and an untiring atheist fight.

These millions should be supplied with the most varied atheist propaganda material, they should be made acquainted with the facts from the most varied spheres of life, they should be approached in this way and in that way, so as to interest them, rouse them from their religious torpor, stir them from the most varied angles and by the most varied methods, and so forth.

Lenin, "On the Significance of Militant Materialism," *Selected Works*, Vol. XI, pp. 72-74.

The magazine *Under the Banner of Marxism,* which sets out to be an organ of militant materialism, must devote a lot of space to atheist propaganda, to reviews of the literature on the subject and to correcting the immense shortcomings of our governmental work in this field. It is particularly important to utilize books and pamphlets which contain many concrete facts and comparisons showing how the class interests and class organisations of the modern bourgeoisie are connected with the organisations of religious institutions and religious propaganda.

Extremely important is all material relating to the United States of America, where the official, state connection between religion and capital is less manifest. But, on the other hand, it makes it clearer to us that so-called "modern democracy" (which the Mensheviks, the Socialist-Revolutionaries, partly also the anarchists, etc., so unreasonably worship) is nothing but the freedom to preach what it is to the advantage of the bourgeoisie to preach, namely, the most reactionary ideas, religion, obscurantism, defence of the exploiters, and so forth.

Lenin, *ibid.,* pp. 75-76.

The philosophy of Marxism-Leninism — the theoretical foundation of the Communist Party — is incompatible with religion. . . . The world outlook of the party is based on scientific data, while religion contradicts science. As the Party bases its activity on a scientific foundation, it is bound to oppose religion.

Young Bolshevik, No. 5-6, 1946, p. 58.

In the educational work of the Party organizations a serious place must be assigned to the fight against religious beliefs and superstitions and to educating the masses in an atheistic world outlook.

M. Poldugolnikov, "Party Meetings — the School of the Bolshevist Education of Communists," *Bolshevik,* July 1950, p. 53.

149

If a Communist Youth believes in God and goes to church, he fails to fulfill his duties. This means that he has not yet rid himself of religious superstitions and has not become a fully conscious person (Communist).

Young Bolshevik, No. 5-6, 1946, p. 56.

A young man or woman cannot be a Communist youth unless he or she is free of religious convictions.

Young Communist Pravda, October 18, 1947.

Spiritual struggle against religion and religious prejudices; it emerges and develops in connection with the growth of class struggle, and with the development of materialistic, scientific knowledge. The necessity of anti-religious propaganda is provoked by the reaction of religious ideology. . . .

Marxist-Leninist anti-religious propaganda entirely unmasks every and all forms of religion, it is a sharp spiritual weapon in the struggle of the working class for progress, for socialism and for communism. . . .

The founders of Marxism-Leninism put anti-religious propaganda on a scientific basis; they made it a component part of the propaganda connected with the dialectical-materialistic world outlook, an irreplaceable part of the proletarian class struggle aimed at the overthrow of the bourgeois order. . . .

Only after the great October socialist revolution in the Soviet Union, were the necessary conditions created for a really large-scale development of Marxist anti-religious propaganda. Science was made the property of the working class; the church was separated from the state and the school from the church. . . .

Anti-religious propaganda in the U.S.S.R. took the character of a mass anti-religious movement. In the anti-religious circles, museums and higher educational institutions as well as in the anti-religious journals, the experience of the anti-religious propaganda is accumulated and further developed; new qualified cadres are activated and educated and investigative thought is promoted. Millions of Soviet people sever their connections with religion and conduct an active anti-religious propaganda. The Communist Party leads continuously

150

this anti-religious propaganda as well as directs the activity of the cultural-educational organizations in this field.

The building up of Socialism in the U.S.S.R. did not eliminate the aim of unfolding the anti-religious propaganda. On the contrary, it raised this aim to a new height. Under the conditions of socialism, there appeared the genuine opportunity to liquidate, once and for all, the religious prejudices, to make all citizens of the U.S.S.R. conscientious builders of Communism. . . .

The struggle for the final overcoming of religious belief is realized by the united effort of all cultural-education, Trade-Union and Comsomol Organizations, with the help of all soviet peoples. . . .

Article: "Anti-Religious Propaganda," *Bolshaya Sovietskaya Enziklopedia,* Vol. II, Second Edition, Moscow, 1950, pp. 511-512.

The genuine scientific theory of militant atheism is presented in the classic works of Marx, Engels, Lenin and Stalin. Marxist-Leninist atheism differs radically from all prior atheisms; it opens a new era in the struggle against religious beliefs. . . .

Contrary to the pre-Marxian atheism which was afraid of the masses and was a world outlook of the "selected," the proletarian atheism as the ideology of millions is the spiritual weapon of the working class in its struggle for a new world — for communism. Proletarian atheism — the materialistic world outlook — triumphed in the country of socialism — the U.S.S.R., and embraces the millions of the working masses throughout the world.

In the new historical conditions, Lenin and Stalin had further developed the atheistic theory of Marxism, they enriched it with the new experiences of the class struggle and socialist construction.

Marxism-Leninism proved irrefutably that the roots of religion are to be found in the material life of society, that the religious views of the society and its appropriate institutions belong into the field of superstructure. . . .

The U.S.S.R. is a country with the atheistic world outlook. Not only the Soviet intelligentsia, the workers of science, culture, technic and arts but also the millions of workers and peasants, the simple factory and farm employers sever their ties with religion. . . .

151

The religious prejudices hinder the religious workingman to understand science and to accumulate knowledge, it hinders his education in the spirit of the Marxist-Leninist world-outlook and prevents him from being a conscientious dependable builder of communism. . . .

The Capitalistic environment makes every effort in order to animate and to support the religious prejudices in the Soviet Union hoping to utilize them for the accomplishment of their imperialistic and aggressive plans. . . .

Article: "Atheism," *Bolshaya Sovietskaya Enziklopedia,* Vol. III, Second Edition, Moscow, 1950, pp. 347-354.

The belief in God, in religion which is the sister of philosophical idealism is characterized by the Marxist-Leninist classics as masked and refined slavery under the clergy. In the same way as the religion regards the World as a creation of God, the philosophical idealism regards the world, as Stalin put it, as the personification of an "absolute idea," "the world spirit," "consciousness." . . .

The dialectical materialism utilizing the achievements of modern natural science, destroys to the ground the idea of God which appears in many refined forms. The liquidation of the religious prejudices and especially the most important of them — the belief in God — presents one of the tasks of the Communist education of the Soviet people.

Article: "God," *Bolshaya Sovietskaya Enziklopedia,* Vol. V, Second Edition, Moscow, 1950, pp. 336-337.

VI. RUSSIAN NATIONALISM AND SOVIET PATRIOTISM

To Comrade Bedny: What is the nature of your error? It consists in the fact that the criticism of defects of living conditions and manners in the U.S.S.R., a criticism, which is required and needed, was developed by you at first quite successfully and skillfully, but later fascinated you beyond measure and by fascinating you it started to grow in your writings to slanders on the U.S.S.R., on its past and its present. . . .

The whole world recognizes now that the center of the revolutionary movement was transferred from Western Europe to Russia. The revolutionaries of all countries look hopefully at the U.S.S.R. as at the center of the liberation struggle of the working class in the whole world, recognizing in it the sole fatherland. The revolutionary working class of all countries applaud single-mindedly the Soviet working class, and, above all, the *Russian* working class, the vanguard of the Soviet workers, as its recognized leader, who conducts the most revolutionary and most active policy, only dreamed by the proletarians of the other countries. The leaders of the revolutionary working class of all countries passionately study the instructive history of the working of Russia, its past, the past of Russia, knowing that beside a reactionary Russia, there existed also a revolutionary Russia, Russia of Radischtschevs, Tshernyshevskis, Zheliabovs, and Ulianovs, Khalturins and Alekseevs. All this inspires (must inspire!) in the hearts of the Russian working class the feeling of a revolutionary national pride, which is able to move mountains, able to perform miracles.

And you? Instead of comprehending this magnificent process in the history of Revolution and to rise yourself to the level of duties of a singer of the leading proletariat, you have started to declare to the whole world, that the Russia of the past represented vessels of abomination and desolation, that the "laziness" and a tendency to "sit on the stove" appear almost as a national feature of the Russians in general, which means also the Russian workers, who by performing the October revolution, of course did not cease to remain Russians. And this is called by you a Bolshevik criticism! No, very honorable Comrade Demian, this is not a Bolshevist criticism but a *slander* on our people, the *dethronation* of the Proletariat of the U.S.S.R., the dethronation of the Russian proletariat.

And you expect after all this, that the C.C. should keep silent! What do you think of our C.C. anyway?

> Stalin, *Sotchinenia*, Vol. XIII, Moscow, 1951, pp. 23-27. This letter, published in 1951, was written in 1930. Bedny was the official Bolshevik poet of the first years of the Soviet regime.

To educate the active fighters for Communism means to teach them to see and appreciate the creative strength and capability of a people, proved by its great historical deeds. The peoples of the

U.S.S.R. under the leadership of the most outstanding among them, the Russian people, have performed the great task of Socialist and cultural development. The Soviet people are rightly proud that with their creative energy, with their revolutionary enthusiasm, under the guidance of the Lenin-Stalin Party they first in the world created the Socialist order. The Soviet people, relying on the indestructible strength of the Soviet regime inspired by the ardent patriotism and consciousness of their great liberation mission under the leadership of its leader, the genius Stalin, did not only save — during the great patriotic war against Hitler's Germany — their freedom, but saved from destruction the whole European civilization. There appeared before the whole world the magnificent features of the Soviet people — courage, daring, clear mind, staunch character, great cleverness.

Enemies of the U.S.S.R. abroad, to whom the greatness of the Soviet country causes hatred and anger, try in every possible way to distort the factual history of culture, are spreading lies that Russian science, techniques, literature, arts, are not "independent" but "imitative" in character. All this is done with the goal to belittle the growing authority of the Soviet Union in the opinion of progressive society and to plant in the minds of the Soviet people the spirit of servility before Western civilization. Whatever the practice of the enemies of the U.S.S.R. should be, they will never succeed in concealing the fact that the great Russian culture contributed enormous independent and many-sided investments in world culture.

This indication by Stalin has a tremendous significance for the struggle against all kinds of servility before the West, for the strengthening of national consciousness of people, for their education in the spirit of Soviet patriotism. The Soviet patriotism is one of the moving powers in the development of our society and it is necessary to constantly strengthen it in order that Soviet society can successfully move forward to newer and higher shapes. That is why the important task of our whole ideological work consists in tireless education of people in the spirit of deep devotion and loyalty to the Soviet motherland.

Editorial about the teaching of Marxism-Leninism in higher educational institutions, *Bolshevik*, No. 5, March 1947, p. 3.

The disdainful attitude toward national consciousness of the nation is one of the manifestations of the ideology of domination of Imperialist states over the colonial and dependent countries. This ideology appears often under the mask of bourgeois cosmopolitanism. Engels explained already that the bourgeois cosmopolitanism is an expression of the expansion of Capitalist domination over the entire world. To the Capitalist, aiming at eliminating his foreign competitor, it is profitable to talk about the so-called cosmopolitanism. It is characteristic that contemporary imperialists struggling for world domination by the English speaking nations very often hide their aggressive desires with the jabbering as though national self-consciousness is an obstacle on the road to peaceful cooperation between nations.

It is comfortable for the Imperialists to undermine the national self-consciousness in order to facilitate for themselves the affirmation of their domination. Marxism-Leninism is hostile to the bourgeois cosmopolitan, called to excuse the domination of the nations by others, suppression of the free development of national cultures, especially their democratic and socialist elements. Bolsheviks are struggling for the blossoming of national cultures, socialist in substance.

Comrade Stalin in his report at the 18th Party Congress branded the crawling and servile fawning of Trotskyites and Bukharinites before the foreign countries and simultaneously underlined that " . . . the last Soviet citizen, free from the menace of Capitalism stays a head higher from any foreign high standing proprietor dragging on his shoulder the yoke of capitalist slavery . . ." It is necessary to educate the Soviet people to be proud of their socialist motherland, for its great people.

> S. Kovalev, "Communist education of the toiling masses and overcoming of the survivals of Capitalism in the consciousness of the people," *Bolshevik,* No. 5, March 1947, pp. 17, 19-20.

At the end of the eighteenth century the Right Bank Ukraine went to Russia and was in this way freed from the oppression of the Polish gentry. In Czarist Russia, the Ukrainians as well as other national groups were also subject to a hard social and national oppression. However, the transition of the Ukraine under the

155

Russian rule was still less evil than the danger of being absorbed by gentry Poland and Sultan Turkey — a danger which was impending at that time over the Ukraine and threatened the Ukrainian people with total destruction of their national existence.

Leninism played a decisive role in the historical destinies of all nations of the former Czarist Russia including the Ukraine. Arising from the stable basis of Leninism, the Bolshevik Party and the Russian working class helped the toilers of the Ukraine to overthrow the landlords and capitalists and establish the Soviet order and the real guarantee of the total social and national liberation. The Ukrainian people struggled during long years for its sovereignty but reaching that goal was possible, thanks only to the victory of the great Russian Socialist Revolution. Only after that victory, in December 1917, a Ukrainian Soviet Socialist Republic was proclaimed. For the creation of the Ukrainian Soviet state a great merit belongs to the Bolshevik Party and its leaders Lenin and Stalin.

The centuries-old dream of the Ukrainian people was realized in the years 1939-1945 by the Soviet government under the leadership of the Bolshevik Party, the great leader, Comrade Stalin. At present Soviet Ukraine totally unites all Ukrainian territories about which the Ukrainian people dreamed for centuries.

Only thanks to the Union, with the Russian people, thanks to its help and the help of other people of the U.S.S.R. the Ukrainian people saved, during the great patriotic war 1941-1945, its independence and its existence as a state.

> K. Litvin, "About the History of the Ukranian People," *Bolshevik,* No. 7, April 1947, pp. 54 f.

In the history of the revolutionary movement of our country, in the struggle for the dictatorship of the proletariat, in the building up of socialism, the significant role in the friendly relations of the people of the U.S.S.R. belongs to the older brother — the great Russian people.

The Russian people gave us Lenin. In the midst of the Russian proletariat, Comrade Stalin, as he himself put it, "learned for the first time what it means to be one of the leaders of the great Party of the working class" (*Sotchinenia,* Vol. VIII, p. 175.)

The Russian people were the first to raise the banner of the Socialist revolution, first to overthrow the rule of capitalists and landlords, to establish the dictatorship of the proletariat and to clear the way for Socialism. All people of our country, learned from the Russian people the fighting and revolutionary traditions.

The brotherly support of the Russian people helped all people of our country to break apart the chains of the bourgeois-landlords' oppression, to establish the Soviet order, to build up the Socialist society.

Under the leadership of the Russian people, the people of the U.S.S.R. are fighting self-sacrificingly for the further blossoming of their Socialist motherland. Comrade Stalin educates the Soviet people in the spirit of gratitude and respect for the great Russian people. The Russian people, Stalin says, appeared to be the most outstanding nation, the leading power of the Soviet Union among all other nations of our country.

M. Bagirov, "The great Leader of Nations," *Bolshevik,* No. 1, January 1950, p. 46.

NOTES

[1] For details cf. F. I. Dan, *Proizchozdenie bolshevisma* (New York, (1946), pp. 273 ff. Valuable also is the earlier book, J. Martov-F. Dan, *Geschichte der russischen Sozialdemokratie* (Berlin, 1926). F. Dan, for years a most influential Menshevik, became during World War II a sympathizer with Bolshevism. For Lenin's report on the second congress cf. *Selected Works,* Vol. II (London, 1936), pp. 341 f. The Stalinist official *History of the Communist Party of the Soviet Union (Bolsheviks)* (New York, 1939) is not a history, but a statement of the official Soviet view on the development of Bolshevism.

[2] The best book on the Third International (Comintern) is that of F. Borkenau, *World Communism, a History of the Communist International* (New York, 1939). Cf. also for its relations with non-Soviet Communist parties Ruth Fischer, *Stalin and German Communism* (Cambridge, Mass., 1948) and Gitlow, *I Confess* (New York, 1940).

[3] A list of such accusations in B. Souvarine, *Staline* (Paris, 1933), pp. 64 f. The Menshevik Axelrod accused Lenin of making men into cogs of a machine. Trotsky wrote in a pamphlet, quoted by Souvarine, *op. cit.,* p. 66, that Lenin's methods would lead to a situation "in which the organisation of the party substitutes itself for the party, the Central Committee for the organisation, and the dictator for the Central Committee."

[4] Dan, *op. cit.,* p. 363, quotes Plekhanov's speech: "As a revolutionary party which tries to reach its ultimate end we must regard democratic principles exclusively from the point of view of realizing as quickly as possible this aim, from the point of view of what is profitable for our party."

[5] Cf. his remarks on primitive dilettantism (*kustarnischestvo*) in the work of Russian Social-Democrats in *Selected Works.* Vol. 11, p. 115. On the influence of Tkachev, and his belief in the necessity of a revolutionary coup d'etat, upon Lenin cf. M. Karpovich, "A Forerunner of Lenin: P. N. Tkachev", *The Review of Politics,* Vol. 6 (1944), 336 f.

[6] Marxian Communism must be clearly distinguished from Ascetic Communism. Marxian Communism has as its aim the maximal increase of pleasures whereas Ascetic Communism regards renunciation of private property as a means to become exclusively concerned with the intellectual and spiritual life. Ascetic Communism is prescribed by Plato for the guardians and, by the vow of poverty, for members of religious communities.

[7] Cf. Stalin, *Dialectical and Historical Materialism* (first published as part 2 of chapter 4 of the official *History* quoted in footnote 1). G. A. Wetter, *Il materialismo dialectico sovietico* (Turin, 1948), and I. M.

NOTES

Bochenski, *Der sowjetrussische dialektische Materialismus* (Bern, 1950); the last book is summarized by its author in the *Review of Politics,* Vol. 13 (1951). Very helpful for the understanding of the philosophical background of Marx' thought and Hegel's influence on Marx is Th. Steinbuechel's collection of articles, *Sozialismus* (Tübingen, 1950). Steinbuechel emphasizes that Marx took over from Hegel the belief in the necessary and reasonable development of history (p. 42). But for Hegel the logic of the spirit immanent in the world is the moving force, whereas for Marx this role is played by "real", material factors.

[8] Cf. E. Voegelin, "The Formation of the Marxian Revolutionary Idea," *The Review of Politics,* Vol. 12 (1950), 275 f., which gives an excellent analysis—with many quotations—of Marx's atheistic views which have been absorbed by Bolshevism. Lenin's anti-religious views can be studied in his *Selected Works,* Vol. XI.

[9] Cf. my article on "Totalitarian Religions," *The Review of Politics,* Vol. 14 (1952), and J. Monnerot, *Sociologie du Communisme* (Paris, 1949). Monnerot shows how the Communist faith in its scientific basis changes science into a dogmatic system which must be enforced by fanatics. These (secularized) pseudo-scientific dogmas do not request prayer and contemplation but are orders for the transformation of the world. "In the name of the dogmas of secular religions human lives are sacrificed to the knowledge which the holders of the 'Truth' possess, knowledge of the ultimate end of history and of the best ways which lead to it." (p. 302). The background of political religions is discussed in E. Voegelin, *Die politischen Religionen* (Stockholm, 1939) and in his monumental *History of Political Ideas* (to be published by Macmillan).

[10] This description of a basic Marxian-Bolshevik belief is not refuted by attempts to give to the superstructures of the economic foundation an increased importance and relative independence, such as Stalin, following many previous interpretations of Marxism, does in his letters on errors in linguistics, *Bolshevik* (Nos. 12 and 14, June and July 1950). There, the role of the Soviet state, of the "revolution from above," is mentioned. J. Ellis and R. W. Davies, "Soviet linguistics," *Soviet Studies,* Vol. II (1951), 163, emphasize correctly the Marxist character of Stalin's statements. Cf. also the article of G. Gleserman in *Bolshevik,* Sept. 6, 1950.

[11] Cf. G. Briefs, *The Proletariat* (New York, 1937).

[12] This distinction between Socialism (which is also called the first phase of Communism) and Communism goes back to K. Marx, "Critique of the Gotha Programme."*Selected Works, op. cit.,* Vol. II, pp. 563 f.

[13] Cf. Stalin's statement on the 18th congress of the Soviet Union Communist Party (CPSU), March 1939; reproduced in English and commented upon by M. T. Florinsky, *Towards an Understanding of USSR* (revised edition, New York, 1951), pp. 17-20; discussed also by A. Vyshinsky in *Sovetskoe Socialistischeskoe Gosudarstvo* (Moscow, 1948), pp. 93 f.

159

14 Stalin, in his report on the Work of the Central Committee to the 18th congress of the CPSU, quoted from Lenin: "We do not regard Marxist theory as something complete and inviolable; on the contrary we are convinced that it has only laid the cornerstone of the science which socialists must further advance in all directions if they wish to keep pace with life. We think that an independent elaboration of the Marxist theory is especially essential for Russian socialists, for this theory provides only general guiding principles which in particular are applied in England differently from France, in France differently from Germany, and in Germany differently from Russia."

15 Lenin, *Selected Works,* Vol. V, preface of 1920, pp. 11 ff.

16 *Ibid.,* p. 9.

17 Lenin defined dictatorship as "power unrestricted by any laws." ("The Proletarian Revolution and the Renegade Kautsky", *Selected Works,* Vol. VII, p. 122).

18 Cf. my article on Lenin's methods of seizing Power in 1917 in W. Conze, ed., Rothfels-Festschriff: *Deutschland und Europa* (Dusseldorf, 1951). For Lenin's three articles against constitutional illusions of August 1917, cf. his works, *Sotchinenia,* (3rd ed. Moscow 1926,) Vol. XXI, pp. 48 f.

19 Karl Marx, "Communist Manifesto," *Selected Works,* Vol. I (New York, International Publishers), pp. 218 f.

20 Cf. E. H. Carr, *The Bolshevik Revolution, 1917-1923,* I (New York, 1951), ch. 2, pp. 26 f. (particularly p. 29 and p. 36); and F. Dan, *op. cit.,* ch. 9, pp. 266 f. (particularly pp. 274-275).

21 Speech at the grave of Karl Marx, March 17, 1883. "Just as Darwin discovered the law of evolution in organic nature, so Marx discovered the law of evolution in human history." Quoted in Marx, *Selected Works,* Vol. I, pp. 1-6.

22 *Op. cit.,* p. 255.

23 *Selected Works,* Vol. VII (London, 1937): "Left Wing childishness and petty bourgeois mentality" (1918), p. 356. "Left Communists are obliged to take refuge behind high sounding and empty phrases. . . . The flaunting of high-sounding phrases is characteristic of the declassed petty-bourgeois intelligentsia."

24 The claim that Marxism is no dogma (rather it is always ready to learn from experience) as well as bitter criticism of such so-called "Marxists" as Kautsky, who knew only the letter of Marx, can be found in many writings of Lenin before and after his seizure of power. Stalin likes to repeat them. Therefore, it is surprising that B. Meissner in his excellent

study *Russland im Umbruch* (Frankfurt, 1951), p. 75, cites a statement of Stalin made in 1950 ["Marxism does not recognize unchangeable formulas. Marxism is hostile to any dogmatism"] in order to show that Stalin has today abandoned his previous Marxism. For a refutation of this view, Cf. the articles of J. Ellis, I. W. Davies and G. Gleserman quoted in footnote 10.

25 Lenin justified the acceptance of the humiliating peace of Brest-Litovsk with the argument that a "respite" was necessary to make a survival of Russia's strength possible. (Cf. his report on "The Immediate Tasks of the Soviet Government" written in March-April 1918, *Selected Works*, Vol. VII, p. 314). A similar argumentation was used in order to justify the replacement of War Communism by the New Economic Policy in 1921.

26 Cf. the wise remarks on this optimism concerning the future in Yves Simon, *Philosophy of Democratic Government* (Chicago, 1951), pp. 2 f. and pp. 116 f.

27 Cf. Marx's *Thesis on Feuerbach* (1845) Thesis XI: The philosophers have interpreted the world in various ways; the point, however, is to change it, Marx, *Selected Works*, Vol. I, p. 475.

28 Pope Pius XI has described in his encyclical against Nazism, *Mit Brennender Sorge* (1937) the misuse of sacred words for this-worldly policies.

29 Cf. K. Loewith, *Meaning in History* (Chicago, 1950), p. 38, about Marx's "philosophy of the proletariat as the chosen people." Cf. also T. Steinbuechel, *op. cit.*, pp. 99 f., article: "The Essence of the Proletariat according to Karl Marx."

30 Barrington Moore has pointed out in his book, *Soviet Politics: The Dilemma of Power* (Cambridge, Mass. 1950), that the realistic means become more and more important than the ends. They can become ends in themselves (the totalitarian state of the present replaces the classless society of the future). But the doctrine with its utopian element, its division of the world into Capitalist devils and Stalinist angels, continues to exercise a great influence when it is required to make a choice in practice among various possibilities.

31 An influential group of writers on the USSR believes in "the existence of a profound organic connection between the Soviet regime and the people of Great Russia." [E. Crankshaw, *Cracks in the Kremlin Wall* (New York, 1951), p. 44.] A few lines after this statement Crankshaw rejects the view "that the Soviet regime is the inevitable expression of the Russian people or that the people as a whole are ardent supporters of the Soviet regime." On the other hand Crankshaw discovers identities between Tsarist and Bolshevik policies and emphasizes that Lenin "should be seen as a

161

Russian first and a Marxian afterwards" (p. 29). His book is directed against the 'propaganda' of such different men as Kerensky, Trotsky, Tito, Krav-chenko and "practically all White Russian exiles" who have one thing in common: good personal reasons for proving that the evils which now afflict Russia and the world are Stalin's evils—and sometimes Lenin's too —and never Russian evils" (pp. 29-30). The views of Crankshaw, which are similar to those expressed by G. Gorer and Margaret Mead, were attacked by S. Hook, in the *New Leader,* New York, 1951.

[32] Cf. S. Kertesz, "Methods of Soviet Penetration in Eastern Europe," in W. Gurian, ed., *Soviet Union* (Notre Dame, 1951).

[33] Cf. W. Gurian, "Changes and Permanence in Soviet Policies," *Thought* (December, 1946).

[34] Only a few books presenting detailed analysis of the Russian intelligentsia and its ideas can be cited: N. Berdyaev, *The Russian Idea* (New York, 1950); T. G. Masaryk, *The Spirit of Russia* (New York, 1919), Sir John Maynard, *Russia in Flux* (New York, 1948), A. von Schelting, *Russland und Europa* (Bern, 1948), A. Koyré, *Etudes sur la Pensée philosophique en Russie* (Paris, 1950). It is regrettable that the work of Ivanov-Razumnik, *Istoria russkoi obshchestvennoi mysli,* "History of Russian Social Thought", (St. Petersburg, 1907) is not available in English.

[35] Cf. F. C. Barghoorn, "D. I. Pisarev: A Representative of Russian Nihilism," *Review of Politics,* Vol. 10 (1948), 196 ff.

[36] H. Kohn, "The Permanent Mission. An Essay on Russia," *Review of Politics,* Vol. X (1948), 267 ff.

[37] An analysis of this book is given by T. G. Masaryk, *The Spirit of Russia,* Vol. II (New York, 1919), pp. 435 ff.

[38] A. Koyré, *op. cit.,* p. 171 ff. and Herzen's memoirs, *My Past and Thoughts* (New York, 1924-1928).

[39] D. Shub, *Lenin, A Biography* (Garden City, 1948), pp. 1 ff.

[40] Lenin emphasized the necessity of "a strongly organized party" in the first issue of the *Iskra* (December 21, 1900) and he developed his views on the party in his book of 1902, *What is to be Done?*

[41] M. Karpovich, *op. cit.,* D. Shub writes: "Lenin was in effect preaching the ideas formulated decades earlier by Peter Tkachev", *op. cit.,* p. 54.

[42] A detailed discussion of this speech in D. Shub, *op. cit.,* pp. 62 ff. At Lenin's insistence, Plekhanov had written in the program draft that the concept of proletarian dictatorship includes "the suppression of all social movements which directly or indirectly threaten the interest of the proletariat."

[43] The best discussion of the polemic about the expropriations, approved by Lenin, is to be found in B. Souvarine, *Staline* (Paris, 1936), pp. 88 ff., where he also gives a detailed description of the Tiflis expropriation of 1907, pp. 93 ff. The official Soviet biographies do not mention these activities of the Soviet leader.

[44] Details of the spies in the Bolshevik party can be found in B. Wolfe, *Three Who Made a Revolution* (New York, 1948).

[45] The classic description of this mentality is given by F. Dostoievsky in his *The Possessed*. An extreme formulation of this mentality is to be found in Nechaev-Bakunin's *Revolutionary Catechism* of 1869. "The revolutionary regards everything as moral which helps the triumph of revolution, soft and enervating feelings of relationship, friendship, love, gratitude, even honor, must be stifled in him by a cold passion for the revolutionary cause. Day and night he must have one thought, one aim —merciless destruction." Quoted by E. H. Carr, *Michael Bakunin,* (London, 1937), p. 380. N. Valentinov has attempted to demonstrate that Tschernyshevsky decisively influenced Lenin's ideal of a revolutionary. See *Novyi Zhurnal,* XXVI and XXVII (1951).

[46] Lenin, *State and Revolution (Selected Works,* Vol. VII, pp. 47 and 61.)

[47] D. Shub, *op. cit.,* p. 130.

[48] Olga Hess Gankina and H. H. Fisher, *The Bolsheviks and the World War* (Stanford, 1940), ch. III.

[49] Later on, Lenin's polemics against Trotsky were cited by Zinoviev and Stalin to show that Trotsky was not a true Bolshevik. Trotsky himself tried to minimize these disagreements—for he humbly regarded Lenin as his teacher, *The Case of Trotsky,* New York, 1937. There he states (p. 49): Lenin "was the teacher, I was the pupil."

[50] Therefore, Lenin had to defend himself against the accusation of being a paid German agent. Germany also permitted the pacifist Menshevik leader Martov to cross her territory.

[51] Stalin, *So-tchinenia,* Vol. VI, pp. 333 f.

[52] Cf. my article in the Rothfels-Festschrift, ed. by W. Conze, *op cit.,* and E. H. Carr, *The Bolshevik Revolution I* (New York, 1950), pp. 71 ff.

[53] M. S. Hrushevsky, *A History of Ukraine* (New Haven, 1941). The liberal Cadet Party, rejecting an agreement reached in the Rada, left the Provisional Government. A. Mazour, *Russia, Past and Present* (New York, 1951), p. 432.

[54] A. Mazour, *op. cit.,* p. 435.

[55] E. H. Carr, *op. cit.,* pp. 93 ff. analyzes the Lenin policies that resulted in the October revolution. Cf. also my article in W. Conze, *op. cit.*

[56] For the text of the decree in English translation, cf. J. H. Meisel and Edward S. Kozera, *Materials for the Study of the Soviet System* (Ann Arbor, Mich., 1950) pp. 19 f.

[57] John W. Wheeler-Bennett, *The Forgotten Peace—Brest-Litovsk* (New York, 1938).

[58] Lenin, *Selected Works*, Vol. VII, pp. 305 f., description of his difficulties in the party in his speech of March 8, 1918. Cf. also my article on "Soviet Foreign Policy" *Yearbook of World Affairs*, Vol. I (London, 1947). Louis Fischer, *The Soviets in World Affairs*, Vol. I (New York, 1930) pp. 13 ff.

[59] Lenin, *Selected Works* VII, " 'Left-Wing' childishness and Petty Bourgeois Mentality", p. 351 f. Lenin writes that one does not have to accept battle against the giants of imperialism; "wait until the conflicts between the imperialists weaken them still more" (p. 353).

[60] The admirer of Lenin, E. H. Carr, *op. cit.*, p. 156, states: "Lenin accepted the terror in principle," though he tried to minimize as "boutade" Lenin's statement: "If (a man) is against (the revolution) we'll stand him up against the wall."

[61] Oliver H. Radkey, *The Election to the Russian Constituent Assembly of 1917* (Cambridge, 1950). For an analysis of Lenin's theses on the Constituent Assembly, cf. E. H. Carr, *op. cit.*, pp. 113 ff.

[62] Lenin, *Sotchinenia* Vol. XXI (3rd ed., Moscow, 1928), p. 194.

[63] M. Dobb, *Soviet Economic Development since 1917* (London, 1948).

[64] Lenin, *Sotchinenia* Vol. XXII (3rd ed., Moscow, 1929), pp. 168 f.

[65] W. H. Chamberlin, *The Russian Revolution, 1917-1921* (New York, 1937); G. Stewart, *The White Armies* (New York, 1933).

[66] F. Borkenau, *World Communism* (New York, 1939).

[67] E. H. Carr, *German-Soviet Relations Between the Two World Wars, 1919-1939* (Baltimore, 1951).

[68] E. H. Carr, *The Bolshevik Revolution I*, pp. 309 ff.

[69] Lenin, *Sotchinenia* Vol. XXVI (3rd ed., Moscow, 1930), p. 588.

[70] Stalin, *Ob opposizii* (Moscow, 1928), p. 226.

[71] That has been recognized by Stalin himself in his warning against dizziness from success. *Sotchinenia*, Vol. XII (Moscow, 1949), p. 191 f.

[72] N. Jasny states: "At gun point, with sacrifices of millions of lives and by sending other millions in concentration camps, almost 100 million peasants and their families were herded into the Kholkhos", *Soviet Studies*, Vol. III, No. 2 (Oxford, October 1951), 161.

[73] Cf. D. Dallin and B. Nikolaevsky, *Forced Labor in the Soviet Union* (New Haven, 1947). Of the many books of former inmates of Soviet camps most revealing is the introductory survey of M. Rozanov's *Zavoevately bielych piaten* (Posev, Limburg, 1951), V-XXXVI.

[74] B. I. Schwartz, *Chinese Communism and the Rise of Mao* (Cambridge, 1951).

[75] With some exaggeration K. Mehnert claims that, with the condemnation of Pokrovsky—after his death (1932)—and the publication of Stalin's and Molotov's decree on teaching history of May 16, 1934, a new period in Bolshevik ideology started. (Cf. his interesting study *Weltrevolution durch Weltgeschichte,* Schriftenreihe der Deutchen Europa Akademie, Heft 9, Kitzingen, 1951). About the persecution of the Pokrovsky School, cf. A. Ouralov, *Staline au Pouvoir* (Paris, 1951) pp. 114-135. Cf. also S. Yakobson, "Postwar Historical Research in the Soviet Union" in Philip E. Mosely, ed., "The Soviet Union Since World War II" (*The Annals of the Academy of Political and Social Science,* Philadelphia, 1949); G. Kagan "La crise de la science historique russe," *Revue Historique,* 1940; G. von Rauch, "Die sowjetische Geschichtsforschung heute," *Die Welt als Geschichte,* XI (1951), Heft 4.

[76] F. L. Schuman, *Soviet Politics at Home and Abroad* (New York, 1946) gives (on pp. 261 ff.) a long though incomplete list of the prominent victims of the purge. "The number of little people who were purged cannot be estimated" (p. 262). On the one hand, F. L. Schuman believes that "the portrait of conspiracy spread on the Soviet court record" is "closer to reality than any alternative explanation" (264); on the other hand, he states: "The Soviet authorities preferred to see a thousand innocents liquidated rather than see a traitor escape." (268) Lists of those who had to be arrested were drawn up according to "objective criteria": membership in non-Communist parties—even before the rise of the Soviet regime, e.g., the security organs received orders to arrest certain percentages of the population. Another feature was the ultimate purge in their turn of the purgers of the first stages. Almost all Caucasian colleagues of Beria, who headed the NKVD in the Caucasus until he became Ezhov's successor, disappeared. Cf. the many books describing the great purge: particularly revealing are A. Ouralov, *op. cit.,* and A. Weissberg, *The Accused* (New York, 1951). Weissberg was a foreign Communist who lived in the USSR as a leading expert in physics.—Three members of Stalin's Politburo disappeared during the purge [G. K. Schueller, *The Politburo* (Stanford, 1951).]

[77] Cf. M. Beloff, *The Foreign Policy of Soviet Russia, 1929-1941,* Vol. I (New York, 1949).

[78] M. Beloff, *op. cit.,* Vol. II (New York, 1950); E. H. Carr, *German Soviet Relations Between the Two World Wars, 1919-1939* (Baltimore, 1951). Source books are *Nazi-Soviet Relations 1939-1941* (Department of

State, Washington, 1948), and Alfred Seidl (ed.), *Beziehungen zwischen Deutschland und der Sowjetunion* (Tübingen, 1949). Cf. also A. Rossi, *The Russo-German Alliance* (Boston, 1951).

[79] In the conflict with Marshal Tito the Cominform (declaration of June 28, 1948) stated that the criticism made by the Central Committee of the Soviet Party must be accepted by the Yugoslav Party. *The Soviet-Yugoslav Dispute* (London, 1948), p. 65.

[80] For the policy of containment cf. G. Kennan, "The Sources of Soviet Conduct," first printed in *Foreign Affairs*, July 1947, reprinted in *American Diplomacy 1900-1950* (Chicago, 1951).

[81] L. Laurat, *Du Komintern au Kominform* (Paris, 1951).

[82] True, the "strengthening" of the ideological front was accomplished systematically under Zhdanov's leadership after world war. But it was not a new policy, as the previous condemnations of the philosophical school of Deborin, the juridical school of Pashukanis and the historical school of Pokrovsky show. A. Werth, though he tries to characterize Zhdanov's activities as temporary exaggerations, writes: "In their decisions Zhdanov and the Central Committee did, in fact, little more than harden Government and Party policy which had, in practice, been pursued for many years." (*Musical Uproar in Moscow*, London, 1949).

[83] This alliance was called a "smytshka." The poor peasants were used by the Soviet government as allies in the fight against the "kulaks," the so-called wealthy peasants. When Stalin organized the collectivization of agriculture, the official Soviet policy counted—differing from the so-called rightist opposition under Bukharin and Rykov—the "seredniaks" (that is, the peasants between the "kulaks" and the poor peasants), among the Kulaks whose domination was to be destroyed by the imposed collectivization. The rightists, willing to be satisfied by taxes and limited deliveries, and believing in a competition between the private and socialized sectors of the economy, rejected the forced collectivization. The collectivized agriculture was made into a part of the economy planned and directed by the state; it also permitted the exploitation of the peasantry forced into the Kholchozes by the government, for it determined the prices of the products whose delivery is imposed. O. Schiller wrote: "The state obtains the greatest part of the products for prices which are far below the prices of the free market or the prices of the consumer goods." By this method a large part of the Soviet budget is financed. "Agriculture . . . pays a decisive contribution for the financing of the economic construction and armament." (Kolchoz und Genossenschaft, *Osteuropa*, Stuttgart, Vol. I, No. 1, October 1951, p. 16). Furthermore, the state controls the Kholchozes by its Motor-Tractor Stations (MTS) which have in their hands all necessary heavy equipment. High prices are charged for the obligatory use of this equipment (p. 15).

[84] Cf. K. Marx, "Critique of the Gotha Programme," *Selected Works II*,

NOTES

pp. 563 ff. What is called by Marx the first phase of Communist society is today called Socialism by the Bolsheviks. Stalin has increasingly emphasized the absence of equality in compensation under Socialism. Cf. his speech of June 13, 1931 where he states: "It is not feasible for a railroad transport engineer to receive the same salary as a typist. Marx and Lenin say that the difference between skilled and unskilled labor will exist under Socialism even after the abolishment of classes." *Sotchinenia*, Vol. XIII (Moscow 1951), p. 57.

[85] Cf. M. Florinsky, *op. cit.* The survival of the state is more and more emphasized by Stalin, whereas its "withering away" is postponed to a far distant future when Communism will be realized everywhere on the globe.

[86] This situation is well characterized by R. Schlesinger, a writer friendly towards Stalin's regime: ". . . the Soviet judge . . . knows that he may often have to sign a warrant for arrest on no other ground than the declaration of the NKVD, that they have serious suspicions of a man and that the public interest prohibits their divulging all the details even to the local judge—and he knows, too, that only in the few cases which are brought to trial before the ordinary court will he ever learn the details. As a Communist and Soviet patriot our friend regards these things as necessary for the defence of his fatherland. But he is judge enough and lawyer enough to include them in his theoretical analysis of the law", *Soviet Legal Theory* (New York, 1945), pp. 12 f.

[87] Cf. Par. 11 and 12 of the New Party Charter accepted by the 18th congress of the Soviet Union Communist Party (March 10-21, 1939), reprinted in J. H. Meisel and E. S. Kozera, *Materials for the Study of the Soviet System* (Ann Arbor, Mich., 1950) pp. 327 f. The resolution accepted by the Congress on the report of Zhdanov (Meisel and Kozera, *op. cit.,* p. 310) proposes in Par. 3 to abolish mass purges in the Party; for they do not permit Party members to be "treated with careful consideration and in practice . . . often lead to the infringement of the rights of Party members." B. Meissner *op. cit.,* (note 24) pp. 7 f. gives a particularly good description of the party and its development under Stalin.

[88] Cf. I. Deutscher, *Soviet Trade Unions. Their Place in Soviet Labour Policy* (London-New York, 1950): "The Soviet trade unions have often been used by the employer-state as an instrument of coercion against the working classes. As the organization designed to forge the workers' solidarity in their struggle for better living conditions, they have suffered complete atrophy. As bodies entrusted with the management of social insurance . . . they have performed as subsidiaries of the State administration, not as autonomous social bodies", (pp. 135 f.).

In the statute of the Soviet Trade Unions (adopted April 27, 1949) it is said that the Unions are voluntary non-party organizations, but they "carry out their entire work under the leadership of the Communist Party."

167

They "rally the working masses behind the party of Lenin-Stalin," (reprinted in Deutscher, *op. cit.*, pp. 141 f.).

[89] Cf. N. S. Timasheff, "Religion in Russia, 1941-1950," in W. Gurian, ed., *The Soviet Union*, pp. 153-194.

[90] On the theories of Pashukanis cf. R. Schlesinger, *op. cit.*, and *Soviet Legal Philosophy*, translated by H. W. Babb with an introduction by John N. Hazard (Cambridge, Mass., 1951). Hazard writes: Pashukanis' "principal difficulties had been with the withering away of the state . . ." (p. 28). "He had thought that law would disappear as the capitalist system was replaced, while the leaders now stated that an accurate interpretation of Marxism required the recognition of the law's continuation, its existence, even after the achievement of socialism" (p. 29).

[91] Article 30 of the (Stalin) Constitution of the USSR adopted on December 5, 1936. Translation in S. N. Harper-R. Thompson, *The Government of the Soviet Union* (New York, 1949), pp. 326 f. J. Towster, *Political Power in the USSR 1917-1947* (New York, 1948) remarks correctly: "Though theoretically the legislating organ . . . the Supreme Soviet has so far operated primarily as a ratifying and propagating body. Its chief purpose appears to be, periodically or as occasion demands, to lend the voice of approval of a representative assembly to governmental policy." (p. 263). Cf. also B. Meissner, *op. cit.*, pp. 59 f.

[92] On the Politburo cf. the study of George K. Schueller (Stanford, 1951); L. Ouralov, *op. cit.*, claims that Stalin purged without the required permission of the majority of the Central Committee which, though Stalinist, hesitated to accept his proposals; the rules against factionalism inside the party and on the exclusion of leading members go back to a decision made upon Lenin's initiative by the party congress of 1921. Cf. Towster, *op. cit.*, p. 125; Yves Delbars, *Le vrai Staline* (Paris, 1950, not always reliable, but utilizing valuable, unpublished source-material.)

[93] Cf. the works of I. Deutscher and B. Souvarine; a brief description of Stalin's rise to power in my article "Stalin," *Hochland*, August, 1951. For description of the opposition to Stalin cf. Towster, *op. cit.*, pp. 130 f.

[94] Cf. the quotation from Stalin's book *About the Opposition* (1928), reproduced by D. Berlin in the Menshevik *Socialistitchesky Vestnik* (New York-Paris, 1951) pp. 211 f. : "You demand the blood of Bukharin. We will not give you his blood; you know it" (p. 226). This sentence is omitted in Stalin's *Works*—for meanwhile Bukharin had been executed.

[95] Life in the USSR would be impossible without the constant violation of laws. On the other hand, these violations can be used for legal justification of arrests and punishments. Cf. the pertinent remarks of M. Rozanov, *op. cit.*, p. XXVII. "GPU is strong—but tufta [violation of laws] is even stronger."

NOTES

[96] Cf. A. Inkeles, *Public Opinion in Soviet Russia* (Cambridge, Mass., 1950). "The Bolshevik position is . . . based on the general assumption that all social institutions should be adapted to and utilized for the attainment of the goals toward which the society in which they operate is striving" (p. 22). For the distinction between propaganda (addressed to a few) and agitation (addressed to many) see pp. 39 ff.

[97] Cf. The polemic against philosophical heretics in his book on *Materialism and Empirio-Criticism*, or his attacks against Kautsky.

[98] I. M. Bochenski, *Der sowjetrussische dialektische Materialismus*, (Bern, 1951). The appendix (pp. 171 f.) gives examples of public confessions of their errors by philosophers.

[99] "The economists have been permitted more autonomy in adapting themselves to the Party line" notes F. Barghoorn, "The Varga Discussion and Its Significance" (*The American Slavic and East European Review*, Vol. VII (1948), 227). The imposition of the official party line forbidding Mendelism and prescribing the views of Lyashenko was made with great harshness.—The best brief description is by G. A. Wetter, "Science in Soviet Culture" in G. La Pira, *The Philosophy of Communism* (New York, 1952.)—Valuable surveys of the imposition of the party line on cultural, artistic and scientific activities are contained in the pamphlets of the Institute for the Study of History and Institutions of the U.S.S.R. entitled *Materials of the Conference of the Emigrée Scholars Convened in Munich on January 11-14, 1951* (Munich, 1951; in Russian, with summaries in English).

[100] Stalin's letters on the linguistic problems, published first in *Pravda, Isvestia* and the *Bolshevik*, and reprinted in a special pamphlet, *Marksizm i voprosy jazykoznania* (Moscow, 1950) were received with extravagent praise in all Soviet publications. A. Chikobava writes about them: "The classic work of Comrade Stalin has an exclusively important significance for the development of social sciences. It mobilizes the scientific thought against a vulgarized marxism . . . dogmatism . . . schematisation . . . shows the extraordinary power . . . of the creative principle of Marxism in any field of science . . . opens the way for a progress of science not yet seen before" (*Bolshevik*, June 1951, p. 28). An article on the discussion of this work of Stalin in the faculties of law in Moscow starts: "The genius of Stalin . . . has opened for all Soviet sciences, and among them for the science of law, wide horizons and solutions of new tasks facing our state" (*Sovietskoe Gosudarstvo i Pravo*, No. 3 [March] 1951).

[101] Cf. the statements and decrees collected in R. Schlesinger, *The Family in the U.S.S.R.* (London, 1949). An excellent survey of the development and changes of Soviet legislation on family, marriage, divorce is given by V. Gsovski, *Soviet Civil Law* (Ann Arbor, Mich., 1948) Vol. I, pp. 111-136. The legislation of the first years regarding "registration as mere evidence of marriage" and giving to *de facto* matrimonial relations

169

"the same legal consequences" as to registered ones [Code for the Russian Socialistic Federative Republic of November 19, 1926] has been radically reversed. "All the recent changes"—particularly the law of July 8, 1944 —"show the Soviet legislators came to realize the importance of a stable family" (p. 124). Divorce is made difficult; it is left "to the unlimited discretion of the Soviet court which is an obedient instrument of government policy" (p. 135) of course opposed to divorce. Children born out of wedlock have no claims against the father. "Abortion has been made a punishable offense in 1936" (p. 120). "The right of testate and intestate succession granted in 1922 only to the surviving spouse, direct descendents and actual dependents of the decedent" (p. 131) has been extended. In the absence of close relatives "a person may bequest his property according to his free choice. The highest fee collected from the estate does not exceed ten per cent." V. Gsovski notes that the present legislation "protecting strong family ties offers, on the other hand, wiser opportunity for the government agencies to interfere with the private life of citizens" (p. 136). Marriage of Soviet to non-Soviet citizens has been forbidden since February 15, 1947.

102 Trotsky, e.g., joins in 1917 the "party to disrupt and destroy it from within" (*op. cit.*, p. 199.). Trotsky tries to reduce "the chances of the (October) uprising to naught" (p. 205). Similarly other opponents of Stalin's policies and victims of his purges, such as Bukharin, Zinoviev, Kamenev, Rykov, and Piatakov, are characterized in this official textbook as traitors and sinners against the party. Their condemnation also results in the blackening of their past.

103 N. Leites, *The Operational Code of the Politburo* (New York, 1951) has emphasized the use of Bolshevik party history in order to establish universal types of behavior recurring everywhere. B. Schwartz, *op. cit.*, gives examples of this use in controversies among Chinese Communists.

104 Particularly revealing among the stories of former camp inmates and deportees is that of M. Rozanov, *op. cit.*

105 Cf. the memoirs of Fedotoff-White (who in 1917 was a Russian naval officer), *Survival through War and Revolution*, (Philadelphia, 1939).

106 V. I. Lenin, "Can the Bolsheviks Retain State Power?" (written on October 14, 1917), *Selected Works*, VI (London, 1936), p. 271. "Russia after the 1905 Revolution was ruled by 130,000 landlords. They ruled by the aid of unremitting violence perpetrated on 150,000,000 people, by subjecting them to endless humiliation, and by condemning the vast majority to inhuman toil and to semi-starvation. "And yet we are told that Russia cannot be governed by the 240,000 members of the Bolshevik Party, governing in the interests of the poor and against the rich. These 240,000 already have the support of not less than 1,000,000 votes of the adult population . . . in the August elections to the Petrograd Duma. And

here we already have a 'State apparatus' of 1,000,000 persons, devoted to the socialist state."

[107] Since its beginning in 1903, and particularly since 1917, Bolshevism has been accused of abandoning Marxism. Lenin's seizure of power in a backward country which had not yet reached the capitalist stage, his land decree of 1917, taken over from the non-Marxian Socialist Revolutionaries, were cited as proofs for his betrayal of Marxian orthodoxy. Similarly, Stalin's policies and statements—for example his letters on philology— are utilized in order to show his abandonment of Marxism. These accusations overlook the combination of the belief in an overall development, discovered first by means of Marxian method, with its flexible element, the acceptance of experience. And this experience is identified with considerations of power. The Bolsheviks like to point out that Marx could not prescribe policies for the socialist era, whose realization had remained unknown to him.

[108] This so-called self-criticism permits making subordinates responsible for failures and shortcomings; it can also be used to justify purges, removals, etc. In many cases self-criticism is organized from above. When anyone does not participate in the self-criticism, he may be pictured as refusing to admit his errors, and to confess honestly his opposition against the party line. Self-criticism is also useful to give the impression of free discussion inside the party. Even members of the Politburo—like Andreyev in 1950—have publicly confessed their "errors." Zhdanov and Stalin regretted the absence of discussion and self-criticism when they imposed the party line on various sciences. Cf. article of J. Ellis—R. W. Davies, quoted in footnote 10, p. 261.

[109] Under Lenin the necessity of learning from capitalist native and foreign experts was emphasized. For the inexperienced masses had much to learn, the Tsarist regime having kept them in ignorance. But under Stalin this attitude changed. Now a new generation educated during the Soviet regime had grown up. The Soviet regime worked successfully. This increased the fear and hostility of the capitalist world, and therefore "vigilance" against foreign class enemies was emphasized. All peoples had now to learn from the Soviet model; and the success of Socialism in the U.S.S.R. was linked up with the Russian historical merits and with qualities in the Russian people which permitted ascribing to them every important invention.

[110] Precisely the comparative weakness of the middle class and of the modern Europeanized business group permitted the rise of the Soviet regime. The collapse of the Tsarist authority threatened the society with complete disintegration; the new external integration took place on the basis of a utopianism believing in the right to use all means to bring about an industrialized society. Socialization and totalitarian control became the necessary means of this process, and thereby instruments of domination by a group which does not know any paternalistic or legal restraints.

BOLSHEVISM: AN INTRODUCTION TO SOVIET COMMUNISM

Power-political considerations changed the sometimes ruthless authoritarian Tsarism, limited by its charismatic-traditionalist basis, into a pure totalitarianism whose doctrinal basis justified its techniques of limitless domination and expansion. The belief in technical industrial progress, made possible through the Bolshevik rule, changed absolutism, a product of Russian history, into a totalitarianism with purely technical and, therefore, inhuman character. The socialist humanitarian origins helped to cover up the reality by propaganda that confused adversaries and attracted many people outside the USSR.

[111] Cf. G. Fedotov, "Russia and Freedom," *Review of Politics,* Vol. 8 (1946), 19 f.; "The Moscow Tsar wanted to reign over slaves. . ." Finally, in the seventeenth and eighteenth centuries "all the classes were tied to the state by personal service or work. Free professions, save brigandry, were unthinkable." "The historic trend in Russia was the reverse of that in western Europe: it was a development from freedom to servitude. This servitude was the outcome not of the rulers' whim but of a new national objective: the creation of an empire upon a very meagre economic basis. Only through tremendous general strain, iron discipline, and gruesome sacrifice could exist this beggarly, barbaric, endlessly expanding Empire."

[112] Cf. Lenin's critical remarks on V. Suchanov's memoirs, *Sotchinenia* (3rd ed., Moscow, 1931), Vol. XXVII, pp. 398-401. Lenin emphasizes that the revolutionary development in Russia did not have to follow western models though he tries to combine his acceptance of the Russian particular way with the general laws of development. He also stresses the decisive importance of the daring exploitation of new, unforeseen conditions and opportunities, and he quotes with approval Napoleon's sentence: "On s'engage et puis . . . on voit." (One starts the battle and then one sees.)

[113] Under Lenin, after the end of the civil war, the so-called workers' opposition had developed, criticizing the bureaucratic Soviet state. The remnants of this opposition were definitively destroyed under Stalin, together with the Trotsky-Zinoviev bloc.

[114] Cf. the description of this fight in Y. Delbars, *Le vrai Staline* (Paris, 1950), pp. 375 f. Characteristic is Stalin's long statement of April 1929 whose full text was published only in his *Sotchinenia,* Vol. XII. (Moscow, 1949). Here Stalin rejects the claim of the rightists that they share with him the same general line. He accuses the rightists of not fighting against the Kulaks.

[115] Cf. the statements of Stalin reprinted in *Soviet Foreign Policy during the Patriotic War* (London, n.d.), Vol. I, June 22, 1941-December 31, 1943.

[116] Typical of the present attitude of the Soviet regime towards the Tsarist past is a letter from the leading Soviet historian, M. V. Netchkina (*Voprosy Istorii,* Moscow, No. 4, 1951). Miss Netchkina praises the incorporation of the Ukraine and the Caucasus region into the Tsarist

172

NOTES

Empire, but at the same time she criticizes the rule of the Romanoffs under which only the estate owners lived well, whereas the masses—even of the Great Russians, though they were a little better off than those of other nations — had to suffer oppression. The official Great Russian nationalism of the present Soviet policy is expressed in such formulations as "the older brother of the peoples, the Great Russian people" (46). In order to evaluate the incorporation of non-Russian peoples into the Empire, it is proposed to consider the positive results "which despite the Tsarist regime the Great Russian people brought to the economic and cultural life of the peoples" (47). The views of the Pokrovsky school, which regarded the incorporation of Georgia and the Ukraine as an absolute evil, are completely rejected.

[117] This evaluation is used in the Stalin biography by I. Deutscher.

[118] Cf. the remarks in Harry Schwartz, *Russia's Soviet Economy* (New York, 1951): "The Soviet people bore the brunt of the cost of Soviet industrialization as did their ancestors in the time of Peter the Great. The impressive production achievements of Soviet heavy industry are unmatched in those sections of the economy serving consumers, except for education and medical care, both fields directly related to production efficiency. The government put guns before butter and factories before homes, failing time and time again to realize the glowing promises of improved conditions made to its people" (p. 537). About the most recent development *The Economist* (London), Vol. CLXII, No. 5659, February 9, 1952, p. 346 states: "The gap between the output of producer and consumer goods has remained since the war as wide as it was before. While basic materials and engineering products exceeded quite stiff production targets and left the 1940 level far behind, the output of many consumer goods just reached the prewar level and often failed to fulfill their very modest targets."

[119] Cf. footnote 108; also the statement of Harry Schwartz: ". . . self-criticism [is] limited, to revealing defects in the way in which government orders are being executed. Basic government policy and the highest officials in the Politburo are immune to such state-approved criticism," *op. cit.*, p. 180.

[120] Cf. the description by M. Rozanov, *op. cit.*, XIII, where this gradation of food rations according to the work accomplished is described in detail. "The stomach determined the labor policy of the camps. The fear of hunger determined the production in the camps, producing the stakhanov groups" (that is, workers with a particularly high production).

[121] The utopian belief in the perfect classless society of the future results in the justification of the maximum of coercion in the present. All those who are opponents, or who are simply declared to be enemies of the regime, can be mercilessly exterminated, for they prevent the realization of utopia. And those in power have unlimited rights, for the power-holders allegedly serve a necessary development towards utopia—and not any personal aims.

[122] As A. Weissberg, *op. cit.*, relying upon his own experience, observes: those arrested during the purge were accused of being enemies of the Soviet regime when they refused to confess the crimes ascribed to them by the MVD—their refusal proved that they rejected cooperation with the regime and actually accused it of lying.

[123] Cf. F. Borkenau, *op. cit.* The leadership of the Third International was afraid that moderate socialist opportunists, "social-patriots" who had sold out to imperialists during World War I, would join the Communist movement; the 21 points containing the conditions under which socialist groups would be accepted by the Third International, were directed against them.

[124] The best surveys of the Civil War between the Red Army and its White opponents are given by W. H. Chamberlin, *op. cit.*, and G. Stewart, *op. cit.*

[125] K. London, *The Seven Soviet Arts* (London, n.d.) notes in his preface, dated 1936-37, that he is an objective liberal observer and states: "In the Soviet Union . . . culture and its reconstruction within a new society, forms one of the most essential interests both of government and people" (p. 5).

[126] K. London, *op. cit.*, regrets that Lenin had no understanding of modern art, but he judged it "with infinitely greater generosity. . . . With the stabilization of Stalin's power the activities of leftist artists were eliminated" (p. 76).

[127] It would be fascinating to write a history of the Bolshevik party and the Soviet regime as a history of the defections which accompany them from their beginnings. Here it is only possible to hint at a general classification of these defections. First, there are those old Socialists and Bolsheviks who were not willing to accept the doctrinal authority of Lenin (e.g. Bogdanov). Some of them returned to the fold, e.g. Lunatscharski, or tried to minimize their disagreements with Lenin, e.g. Trotsky after 1917; later he accused Stalin of having betrayed Lenin and true Bolshevism. Secondly, there are those who are disappointed with the policies of the regime; afraid of being purged, they refuse to return to the U.S.S.R. —such officials as Agabekov (former Tcheka-leader) and such Soviet diplomats as Bessedovsky and Dmitrievsky. Many of them became nationalist opponents of the anti-Russian Soviet regime—e.g. General Vlasov, who, after having become a German prisoner, tried to organize during World War II, a national Russian army. Third, there are disappointed intellectuals, artists, social reformers and socialists. Typical of the rejection, of the original strange belief that the Soviet regime is realizing humanitarian needs, is the attitude of André Gide. This realization of radical misunderstanding of the Soviet regime may result in the sharpest criticism of a gullible western world and of all "liberals" and "progressives" who are unable to oppose the U.S.S.R. energetically and to fight the Communist

NOTES

poison everywhere. Some ex-Communists, e.g., M. Eastman, reject all socialism, whereas others, like Silone, continue to accept it in a humanitarian-democratic form. The belief that all ex-Communists retain the mentality peculiar to adherents of political religions (though of course abandoning Communist contents) is not proved by facts; true some do apply the fanatical intolerant attitude of their communist days against everyone who does not now agree with them.

[128] R. Schlesinger, *The Family in the U.S.S.R.* (pp. 391 f.) tries to prove that the return to more conservative views on marriage and family was the consequence of a peculiar situation—the losses in the war forced emphasis on an increase of the birth rate. The Soviet leadership of today does not care about the opinion of progressive intellectuals where considerations of power are involved. Stalin continues Lenin's stress on the need to maintain the existence of the Soviet regime and not to sacrifice it to utopian slogans which do not take into account existing power conditions.

[129] Therefore, the pro-Soviet Socialist Unity party has very much declined in Eastern Germany. Too much actual experience opposed the Communist propaganda. That the mass following of Communism in France and Italy has not been substantially reduced, can be explained by the absence of a mass experience with Communist rule.

[130] This is the basic attitude of E. H. Carr. He is impressed by the power political aspects of the Soviet regime, not by its doctrine or by its progressive propaganda claims.

[131] An excellent summary of Soviet attitudes towards national groups is to be found in S. M. Schwarz, *The Jews in the Soviet Union* (Syracuse, 1951).

[132] On the Ukrainian problem cf. the article of M. Pap, *The Review of Politics*, Vol. 14 (April 1952) and John S. Reshetar, Jr., *The Ukrainian Revolution* (Princeton, 1952).

[133] E. H. Carr, *The Bolshevik Revolution, 1917-1923,* I, particularly chs. 13 and 14.

[134] Of the many studies about Tito and Titoism Adam B. Ulam, "The Background of the Soviet Yugoslav Dispute," *The Review of Politics,* Vol. 13 (January 1951), and H. F. Armstrong, *Tito and Goliath* (New York, 1951) may be cited in particular.

[135] On the Soviet satellites cf. the article of S. Kertesz, "The Plight of Satellite Diplomacy," *Review of Politics,* Vol. 11 (January 1949), pp. 26-62, and "Methods of Soviet Penetration in Eastern Europe," *The Soviet Union,* ed. by W. Gurian (Notre Dame, 1951), pp. 85-136.

[136] Cf. W. Gurian, "The Sources of Hitler's Power," *The Review of*

175

Politics Vol. 4 (October 1942) 379-408; and Don Luigi Sturzo, *"Italy and Fascism"* (New York, 1927.)

[137] Cf. A. Mohler, *Die konservative Revolution,* (Stuttgart, 1951).

[138] Cf. The articles of S. Kertesz, "The Methods of Communist Conquest: Hungary 1944-1947," *World Politics,* Vol. III (October 1950), 20-54, and of Ivo Duchacek, "The Strategy of Communist Infiltration: Czechoslovakia, 1944-1948," *World Politics,* Vol. II (April 1950), 354-373, and "The February Coup in Czechoslovakia," *World Politics,* Vol. II (July 1950), 511-532.

[139] Cf. M. Einaudi-J. M. Domenach-A. Garosci, *Communism in Western Europe* (Ithaca, 1951).

[140] F. Borkenau, "The Comintern in Retrospect," *Dublin Review,* Vol. 213 (July-Sept. 1943).

[141] Bolshevization is the purpose of the purges in non-Russian communist parties. Their leadership has to be composed of men completely subservient to Moscow.

[142] Cf. his formulations in the letter to Comrade Ivanov of February 12, 1938, where he emphasizes that the victory of socialism in the U.S.S.R. can be complete only after Socialism has triumphed also outside of Russia. "It is necessary to strengthen and consolidate the international ties between the working class of the U.S.S.R. and the working class of the bourgeois countries" *Strategy and Tactics of World Communism* (Washington, 1948) p. 158.

[143] Cf. Lenin's *State and Revolution,* where it is announced that democracy will also disappear in the classless and stateless society.

[144] Cf. the remarks of Charles Boyer, S.J., about the contributors to his volume, *The Philosophy of Communism* (New York, 1952). "In denouncing Communism none went so far as to advocate non-Communism" (p. vii).

BIBLIOGRAPHICAL NOTE

A few of the most important books in English are listed.

Background and History

N. A. Berdyaev, *The Origin of Russian Communism,* New York, 1937.
N. A. Berdyaev, *The Russian Idea,* New York, 1948.
G. Fedotov, "Russia and Freedom," *The Review of Politics,* Vol. 8, No. 1, January 1946, pp. 12-36.
M. S. Hrushevsky, *A History of Ukraine,* New Haven, 1941.
M. Karpovich, *Imperial Russia, 1801-1917,* New York, 1932.
H. Kohn, *Panslavism,* Notre Dame, 1952.
J. Mavor, *An Economic History of Russia,* New York, 1925.
Sir J. Maynard, *Russia in Flux,* New York, 1948.
A. G. Mazour, *Russia: Past and Present,* New York, 1951.
B. Pares, *A History of Russia,* New York, 1944.
B. H. Sumner, *A Short History of Russia,* New York, 1943.
G. Vernadsky, *History of Russia,* 3rd ed., New Haven, 1951.

General Problems

E. H. Carr, *The Bolshevik Revolution,* I. and II, New York, 1951 and 1952.
W. H. Chamberlin, *The Russian Revolution, 1917-1921,* New York, 1935.
D. J. Dallin, *The Real Soviet Russia,* New Haven, 1947.
W. Gurian, *Bolshevism: Theory and Practice,* New York, 1932.
W. Gurian, ed., *The Soviet Union: Background, Ideology, Reality,* Notre Dame, 1951.
B. Moore, *Soviet Politics: The Dilemma of Power,* Cambridge, 1950.
Philip E. Mosely, ed., "The Soviet Union since World War II," *The Annals of the Academy of Political and Social Science,* 1949.
F. L. Schuman, *Soviet Politics, at Home and Abroad,* New York, 1946.
N. S. Timasheff, *The Great Retreat,* New York, 1946.
J. Towster, *Political Power in the U.S.S.R., 1917-1947,* New York, 1948.

Biographies

I. Deutscher, *Stalin,* New York, 1949.
D. Shub, *Lenin,* New York, 1948.
B. Souvarine, *Stalin,* New York, 1949.
B. D. Wolfe, *Three Who Made a Revolution,* New York, 1948.

Economics

A. Feiler and J. Marschak, *Management in Russian Industry and Agriculture,* New York, 1944.
H. Schwartz, *Russia's Soviet Economy,* New York, 1951.
N. Jasny, *The Socialized Agriculture of the U.S.S.R.,* Stanford, 1949.

BOLSHEVISM: AN INTRODUCTION TO SOVIET COMMUNISM

Foreign Policy

M. Beloff, *The Foreign Policy of Soviet Russia,* 2 vols. New York, 1947-1949.

D. J. Dallin, *Soviet Russia's Foreign Policy, 1939-1942,* New Haven, 1942.

L. Fischer, *The Soviets in World Affairs,* New York, 1930.

G. Kennan, *American Diplomacy, 1900-1950,* Chicago, 1951.

Forced Labor and Purges

M. Buber, *Under Two Dictators,* London, 1949.

D. J. Dallin and B. I. Nicolaevsky, *Forced Labor in Soviet Russia,* New Haven, 1947.

E. Lipper, *Eleven Years in Soviet Prison Camps,* Chicago, 1951.

E. Weissbrod, *The Accused,* New York, 1951.

Government

S. N. Harper, *The Government of the Soviet Union,* 2nd ed., New York, 1950.

Law

V. Gsovsky, *Soviet Civil Law,* 2 vols., Ann Arbor, 1948.

J. Hazard, ed., *Soviet Legal Philosophy,* Cambridge, Mass., 1951.

R. Schlesinger, *Soviet Legal Theory, Its Social Background and Development,* New York, 1945.

Marxism

I. M. Bochenski, "On Soviet Philosophy," *The Review of Politics,* Vol. 13, July 1951, Notre Dame, pp. 344-353.

S. Hook, *From Hegel to Marx,* New York, 1936.

R. N. C. Hunt, *The Theory and Practice of Communism,* London, 1950.

K. Loewith, *Meaning in History,* Chicago, 1949.

R. Schlesinger, *Marx: His Time and Ours,* London, 1950.

E. Voegelin, "The Formation of the Marxian Revolutionary Idea," *The Review of Politics,* Vol. 12, July 1950, pp. 275-302.

Third International

F. Borkenau, *World Communism: A History of the Communist International,* New York, 1939.

R. Fischer, *Stalin and German Communism,* Cambridge, 1948.

Ex-Communists

R. Crossman, ed., *The God that Failed,* New York, 1951.

B. Gitlow, *I Confess,* New York, 1940.

D. Hyde, *I Believed,* New York, 1950.

BIBLIOGRAPHICAL NOTE

Propaganda

F. C. Barghoorn, *The Soviet Image of the United States*, New York, 1950.
A. Inkeles, *Public Opinion in Soviet Russia*, Cambridge, 1950.

Religion

N. S. Timasheff, *Religion in Soviet Russia, 1917-1942*, New York, 1942.

Documents

J. Bunyan and H. H. Fisher. The *Bolshevik Revolution 1917-1918, Documents and Materials*, Stanford, 1934.
J. Degras, *Calendar of the Soviet Documents on Foreign Policy, 1917-1941*, New York, 1948.
J. Degras, *Soviet Documents on Foreign Policy*, Vol. 1, New York, 1951.
O. Gankina and H. H. Fisher, *The Bolsheviks and the World War; the Origin of the Third International*, Stanford, 1940.
F. A. Golder, *Documents of Russian History, 1914-1924*, New York, 1927.
J. H. Meisel and E. S. Koziera, *Materials for the Study of the Soviet System*, Ann Arbor, Mich., 1950.

Bibliography

P. Grierson, *Books on Soviet Russia, 1917-1942*, London, 1943.

Periodicals

The American Slavic and East European Review, Menasha, Wisconsin, 1945——.
The Annals of the Ukrainian Academy of Arts and Sciences in the U. S., New York, 1951——.
The Current Digest of the Soviet Press, New York, 1949——.
The Russian Review, New York, 1941——.
The Slavonic and East European Review, London, 1922——.
Soviet Press Translations, University of Washington, Seattle, 1944——.
Soviet Studies, a Quarterly Review of the Social and Economic Institutions, of the U.S.S.R., Oxford, 1949——.
The Ukrainian Quarterly, Ukrainian Congress Committee of America, New York, 1944——.

Communist "Classics"

History of the Communist Party of the Soviet Union (Bolsheviks), Short Course, edited by a Commission of the Central Committee of the CPSU (B), New York, 1939.
V. I. Lenin, *Selected Works*, 12 vols., London, 1936-1938.
K. Marx, *Selected Works*, 2 vols., New York, 1936-1937.
J. Stalin, *Leninism*, 2 vols., New York (n. d.).

BOLSHEVISM: AN INTRODUCTION TO SOVIET COMMUNISM

Translations of Works by Soviet Scholars

P. I. Liashchenko, *History of the National Economy of Russia to the 1917 Revolution*, New York, 1949.

A. I. Vyshinsky, *The Law of the Soviet State*, New York, 1948.

A. I. Vyshinsky, *The Teachings of Lenin and Stalin on Proletarian Revolution and the State*, London, 1948.

Anti-Stalinist Polemics

L. Trotsky, *Revolution Betrayed*, New York, 1937.

INDEX

Academy of Science, 66
Adler, Victor, 34
Alexander II, reign of, 28
Alexander III, 29
Allies, Bolshevik appeal for armistice negotiations rejected by, 40
aid to the White Russia armies, 43
Soviet Union on the side of, 53
Anti-imperialist imperialism, 87
Anti-imperialist, Lenin as, 10, 12
Anti-Bolshevik totalitarianism, 91
Anti-Marxian movements, 90
Anti-Tsarist revolutionary movement, 56
Asia, European-American influence in, 89; Bolshevik propaganda in, 96
Asiatic nationalities, 12; rise of, 54
Atheism, 21
Atlantic Pact, 54
Austria, 34, 36
Austrian Socialists, 34
Avenarius, doctrine of, 31
Bakunin, 26
Balkans, Soviet control of, 53
Baltic States, and the Soviets, 44
recognition of independence by Soviet government, 44
Bavaria, Soviet regime in, 44
Belinsky, 26, 28
Berdyaev, 26, 28
Berlin, treaty of, 49
Bluecher, Marshal, disappearance of, 51
Bochenski, 9
Bogdanov, 30
Bolshevik atheism, 6, 21
Bolshevik, Central Committee, 31; Duma, 31; overthrow of Provisional Government, 39; propaganda and activity, 19, 36, 37, 93; purposes, 33; doctrine, capacity of, 3, 7, 8, 16; movement, 2; dangers of, 5; faith, 18; organization of Petrograd, 36; practice, 21; state, 20; system, 25; tactics, 93; theories, 22
Bolshevik Party, 12, 15, 32, 34, 37; rise of, 36, 38, 55, 67, 68; leaders, 17; (see Communist Party) distinguished from uptopian revolutionary movement, 70; and the utilization of auxiliaries, 78
Bolshevik regime, maneuvers of, 46; and terrorism and legal security, 57; and opposition, 73; critiques

of the, 78; and its anti-imperialism, 87
Bolshevik terror, inside the party, 63
Bolsheviks (see Communists), 12, 13, 14, 22, 31, 37; as revolutionary intellectuals, 34; deputies in the Duma of 1912, 34; first attempt to come to power, 38; failure to win majority in elections, 42; conquered Russia, 60; separate organization of, 1; seized power in Russia, 1, 22; views of all other doctrines, 5; religion of, 6; split between Bolsheviks and Mensheviks, 30
Bolshevism (see also Communism), 8, 9, 10, 12, 13, 14, 16, 20, 21, 25, 36; the origin of, 1, 2; the meaning of bolsheviki and mensheviki, 1; father of, 1; name of, 2; Western and Russian aspects of, 2; theory and practice of, 3; Russian reality of, 3; analysis of, 3; world influence, 4; success of, 4; defeat of, 4; as social and political religion, 5; basic doctrine of, 5; denial of God's existence by, 6; God according to, 6; against religion, 6; in action, 17; strength, 18; characteristics of, 22; Soviet reality of, 25; Russian background of, 25; founder of, 33; doctrinaire utopianism of, 46; and Russian nationalism, 55; in the Russian environment, 71; in Russia, 72; rise of, 76; as world power, 83, 84; as political secular pseudo-religion, 83; and socialism, 84; experiences and methods of, victory of, 89; and national socialism and fascism, 91; revolutionary phraseology of, 91; and immanentism, 91; reasons for the world success of, 92; myth of, 98; roots in the west of, 101; political and military problem, 102; a world danger, 104
Bolshevist politics and Russian muscovite history, 56
Brest-Litovsk, treaty of, 40, 46; acceptance by Bolsheviks of, 40; annulment of, 41; acceptance by Lenin, 42; and world revolution, 45

181

INDEX

Ezhov, disappearance of, 51; Ezhovs-china, 51
Fascism, 20, 89; connection between National Socialism and, 91; and the Duce, 91; doctrine of, 92
Feuerbach, 20
Finland, end of civil war, 40; Communists lost control of the police in, 94; and USSR, 94
Fisher, Ruth, 95
Fourth International, unimportant; sectarian affairs, 97
France, military alliance with Soviet Union, 50; split of old socialist party in, 85; Communists expelled from cabinet in, 94
French Revolution, 26; socialists, 35
Galicia, an offensive in, 38
Georgia, Georgian socialists, 31; Menshevik Republic of, 44
German, 9, 11, 26; socialists, 35; independent socialists of Halle, 2; general staff, 37; Social Democratic Party, 35
Germany, imperial, 35; collapse of imperial, 37, 40; disappearance of imperial, 43; of William II, 35; armistice with Bolshevik regime, 40; and Brest-Litovsk Treaty, 40; power in Brest-Litovsk period, 45; collapse of, 44; Soviet attempt to establish Communist domination in, 45; establishment of Hitler's Nazi regime in, 50; aid to Finland, 40; and Soviet regime, 40; military force in Russia, 40; military defeat, 53; support of White Armies, 43; policy of German Foreign Office, 43; and treaty of Rapallo, 45; split of socialist party, 85; national socialist movement in, 90; of Weimar Republic, 90; defeat in, 90; Bolshevik expectation of revolution in, 94; utilization of nationalism by Soviets in, 96; aggression against Poland, 52
Gitlow, 95
God, 5, 6, 20; communist interpretation of, 102
Gogol, 28
Gorki, 6
Gomolka, 93
G. P. U., rechristened Che-ka, 46;

change in the activities of, 48
Hapsburg dual monarchy, collapse of, 44
Hegel, 9, 10, 13; Hegelian philosophy, 10, 91
Herzen, 26; old opponent of Tsarism, 28
Hilferding, 11
Hitler, 54, and Munich, 52; attack on Soviet Union, 53
Hitler's Germany, turn of the Soviet Union to, 50; Soviet fear of an attack by, 52
Historical process, 110
Hobson, 11
Hrushevsky, 47
Hungary, Soviet regime in, 44; purges in, 93; Soviet republic in, 94; Soviet and Hungarian Communists, 93
Hunger catastrophe of 1922, 46
Idealism, 9
Imperialism, 10, 11, 12, 16, 18, 22; imperialists, 14, 35; reason for Lenin's book on, 36; Soviet attack upon, 89, 117
International relations, 10, 11
Iskra (Spark), 29, 32, 78
Italy, liberal-democratic regimes in postwar, 90; Italian Fascist totalitarian movement, 90; Communists expelled from cabinet in, 94
Ivan the Terrible, 56
Jagoda, head of the political police, 51
Jagorov, Marshal, disappearance of, 51
Japan, Soviet policy toward, 49
Jasny, 79
Jesus Christ, 5
Jewish Socialist Bund, 1; Jews and Nazis, 90
Kamenev, 36, 39, 47; made startling public confession, 50; execution of, 51, 12; cooperation with Stalin, 62; expelled from party, 62
Karakhan, execution of, 51
Kautsky, 8, 35
Kerensky 38, end of Kerensky rule, 39; attempt to reconquer Petrograd, 39
Khvostism, heresy of, 67
Kienthal, conference at, 35
Kireyevsky, 26
Kirov, assassination of, 51, 62
Korea, local war in, 54; Soviet arms

183